~Victorian~
Cornwall

Jack Ingrey was an incredible man. From lowly stock in a very small Cornish village, he worked hard at school and gained a scholarship to Harley Grammar School in Bodmin—quite a feat at the time. Jack always lived in St Merryn and was very proud of his village and its people; the surrounding wildlife fascinated him. He was forever taking photos of anything that caught his eye to be included in one of his regular village slideshows. Jack also wrote and directed an annual pantomime, which he took on tour locally; it always sold out—a great credit to his skills as a writer. Among his other talents, Jack wrote local history books, which are still selling to this day. Jack was my best friend and mentor; Jack's early life has been immortalised in With a Pasty in my Packet, *an autobiography co-authored by Jack and myself. I owe my enthusiasm for local history to Jack and*
I am proud to dedicate this book to him.

~*Victorian*~ *Cornwall*

A LOOK AT CORNWALL THROUGH THE EYES OF OUR FOREFATHERS

Malcolm McCarthy

FONTHILL

Fonthill Media Language Policy

Fonthill Media publishes in the international English language market. One language edition is published worldwide. As there are minor differences in spelling and presentation, especially with regard to American English and British English, a policy is necessary to define which form of English to use. The Fonthill Policy is to use the form of English native to the author. Malcolm McCarthy was born and educated in Cornwall; therefore, British English has been adopted in this publication.

Fonthill Media Limited
Fonthill Media LLC
www.fonthillmedia.com
office@fonthillmedia.com

First published in the United Kingdom and the United States of America 2018

British Library Cataloguing in Publication Data:
A catalogue record for this book is available from the British Library

ISBN 978-1-78155-719-8

Typeset in 10pt on 13pt Sabon
Printed and bound in England

Foreword

In 1977, I left my beloved Padstow for the big smoke as a nineteen-year-old who had been mollycoddled at home. To fight my homesickness and also fuel my love of local history, I started collecting postcards of my native town and district; these were readily available at regular postcard fairs. I collected for nearly forty years, then after reading Professor Charles Thomas's scholarly work on early Cornish photography, *Views and Likenesses*, I was inspired to expand my collection; my passion now began encompassing early Cornish photos. I marvel at the atmosphere of these images, but I also like to ponder on the lives of those long dead souls.

With the dawn of photography in 1839, the art quickly spread across the Duchy; it was encouraged by the Royal Polytechnic Society, who ran annual photographic competitions. Due to the cumbersome nature of the equipment, most photographers worked within studios or from home. When you consider the size, weight, and awkwardness of the early cameras, it is not surprising that many did not venture outside of their studios where they made a good livelihood from portraiture. I have not included many portraits in this book as I am sure people interested in Victorian Cornwall would rather see views than people; the exceptions I have made are the very early portraits of members of the Andrew family of Porthcothan in St Eval parish as an illustration of early portraiture, any other portraits included will be of people of particular interest.

The dawn of photography coincidentally collided with the early days of tourism. Cornwall is famous for its beautiful coastal scenery, beaches, and the rock formations of the Land's End district; consequently and unfortunately, the majority of alfresco early Cornish photographs produced by these entrepreneurial photographic artists tended to be of cliffs and rocks. Commercial photographs were produced generally in four paper formats: cartes de viste, which are roughly the size of cigarette or tea cards mounted on thin gauge card and known as CdVs; studio cards, which were approximately 7 by 5 inches mounted on stiff card; stereoviews, which were two photographs approximately 3 inches square mounted on one piece of card and studied through a bifocal viewer to give a 3D image; and albumen prints, which were on very thin paper and designed for pasting in an album and produced in a wide variety of sizes. There are also other early types of images not produced on paper; two are known by the names daguerreotypes and ambrotypes, these are so rare (other than as portraits) that there are only a couple of examples in this book:

This ambrotype portrait is of a member of the Andrew family of Trevethan Farm, Porthcothan, probably taken by Edwin Docton of Padstow in the early 1850s. It portrays a mother with her dead child. This may appear a little morbid to us but was quite a common practice among those who could afford it. This photograph illustrates the metal surround and velvet interior, the outside edge being the wooden box, which has a hinged lid, so it can be completely closed and sealed for protection. The boxes had a small ring, so the image could be hung up, or the box could be partially opened so that they could be freestanding or closed and carried in the pocket as a memento.

Another larger ambrotype believed to be by Edwin Docton of Padstow, also taken in the early 1850s, again depicting a finely dressed male member of the Andrew family from Trevethan Farm, Porthcothan. This photo was not in a cased mount as the previous one but framed. The portrait was mounted in an oval metal frame and was then further mounted on card with an exterior oblong metal frame complete with hanging ring. This portrait is a couple of years earlier than the previous image of a lady and child, but it illustrates perfectly that photographers, even at that early date, were offering different options to their customers.

the Andrew portraits (opposite) and the view of Padstow Post Office (page 56). Daguerreotypes are images captured on a copper plate with silver nitrate and Ambrotypes are captured on glass with a black varnish back; both formats were presented in ornate metal surrounds protected in a velvet-lined wooden case and are difficult to distinguish from each other from the front. Another format that did not involve paper and tended to be late in the Victorian era are photographic glass magic lantern slides; these were a pair of square glass sheets with an image sandwiched between them, a few are included in this book.

As with my last book *Lost Cornwall from Magic Lantern Slides*, I have taken the reader around the county, starting on the north coast and working around to the south coast. Every effort has been made to cover the majority of the county in this book, but I have concentrated where possible on the earlier images as I believe that they need recording; these early images are precious and are treasures to be looked after and preserved for future generations. In this throwaway society, so much of our history is being destroyed without a thought for the future, so every effort must be made to preserve what survives.

I make no apology for the concentration of photographs of certain areas; this is because either the early photographer lived and worked in that area, or it was a popular tourist destination. All the photographs in this book are selected from original prints in my personal collection. I have spent countless hours researching the photos and relied on so many people's local knowledge to help me identify and provide information for the captions, this being done in the spirit of 'gather up the fragments', as the Federation of Old Cornwall Societies motto reads.

I hope that this small selection of images brings you some enjoyment and a little education, but please spare a thought for the hard times that our Cornish ancestors had to endure in their day to day lives just to survive and raise our forefathers; without them, we would not be here.

Malc McCarthy
taclowcoth@aol.com

This is a very early photographic stereoview depicting North Street in Lostwithiel. In 1840, John Barron is listed in *Pigot's Directory* as 'Cabinet Maker'. The one-storey building on the right says on the signboard 'cabinet maker'; we have no address for John Barron, but if this was his shop in North Street, it had gone by 1856 when we have the first *Kelly's Directory*, suggesting this photo could be from before 1856. On the left is the Royal Talbot Hotel; this was not listed in the 1840 directory, but it is listed in the 1856 *Kelly's*.

Acknowledgements

As with my last book, I am heavily in debt to so many people for so much valuable information. I started a Facebook page called 'Unidentified Cornish photos', which provided a fantastic amount of information from local people about old photographs I had in my collection that I knew nothing about, in most cases not even knowing where they were. Local knowledge in my opinion cannot be beaten, and I owe so much to the eager members of the Facebook page who would reply within minutes of a new photo being posted. I would like to make the point that the object of the page is to identify the location of photographs; to date (with the exception of a couple of images), they have all been posted by me, so please visit the page and if you have any photos that baffle you that have a Cornish origin, feel free to post them as it is a great tool so please use it.

Apart from my social media success, I have many people to thank for help in compiling this book. The first is James Plater, who is a marvel at cleaning and repairing old photos; he has worked on most of the photos in this book, taking out marks, improving the contrast, and just generally making them easier to see. He has a website: cherishedcollection.com/samples.htm. John McWilliams has been my go-to guy with any maritime questions or Penzance queries; Paulett Vanhove has been very helpful walking around Gulval looking for buildings. Louise Hayward is my go-to gal for Falmouth questions; and mining questions have been answered by Tony Brooks and Pete Joseph. I thank all these people and many more around the Duchy that I have pestered with emails trying to make the information in this book as accurate and informative as possible.

There will follow an alphabetical list of people who have provided information; many have been the first person to identify a photograph on the 'Unidentified Cornish photos' page. I am humbled by the help I have had and am under no illusion that without the generous help of others, I could not have undertaken this task; thank you one and all: Ally Atkinson, Amelia Bray, Anita Rutherford, Andrew Wilcocks, Andrew Craze, Andrew Langdon, Angela Blakeway, Angela Dickens, Anne Knight, Ann Lenten, Anna Sawahla, Anthony Ball, Anthony Robson, Barry Swabey, Beverly Morgan, Bodmin Town Museum, Bonnie Bouckam, Brian Murrish, Bruce Hunt, Cam Longmuir, Carol Harris, Carole Catterall, Catherine May, Charles Daniel, Chas Wenmoth, Cheryl Rail, Chris Timms, Chris Valle, Chris Walker, Clive Tilley, Craig Truscott, Darren Barker, Darren Hocking, Darren Strick, Dave Rogers, David Barnicoat,

David Eddy, David Thomas, David Thorn, David Watkinson, Dawn Phillips, Dee Edwards, Diane Donahue, Edwina Hannaford, Elizabeth Carne, Fiona Blewett, Francis Gist, Gemma May, Geoff Barter, Geoff Provis, George Barnes, George Hamilton, Gerry Bloomfield, Giles Thomas, Gordon Fielder, Graham Wood, Harold Thomas, Heather Lee, Helen Best, Ian Delve, Ian Dudley, Ian Polmear, Ian Valentine, Ian Williams, James Gossop, Jane Bertuchi, Jane Tutle, Janet Axon, Janet Johnson, Liam Nankervis, Linda Rob Burton, Linda Trevethan, Linda Wilton-Farness, Liz Grant, Liz Harman, Liz Hocking, Lora Winkett, Loraine Beard, Louise and Nigel Haywood, Luke Chown, Lynne K. Mayers. Maggie Perkins, Malcolm Dyer, Marcus Coad, Margaret Thompson, Mark Camp, Mark Scott, Martin Mason, Matthew Stevens, M. D. Hatwood, Melanie Huggins, Merv Davey, Meryl Delve, Michael Van Clark, Michele Townsend, Mick Bonner, Mick Franklin, Mick French, Mike Harcum, Mike Hewitt, Mike Squires, Mike Webber, Mr Salmon from St Mabyn, Myra Cordingly, Newlyn Archive, Nigel Blake, Pam Ettridge, Pam Lomax, Pat Miller, Paulette Vanhove, Pete Joseph, Peter Cogar Pollard, Peter Tonkin, Phil Rodda, Philip Gee, Rachel Burgery Horton. Ray Boyd, Richard Fletcher, Richard Stevens, Rick Cornwall, Rob Atkinson, Robert Adams, Robert Taylor, Robin Chiffers, Robin Turner, Rodney Bate, Roger Collins, Roger Pyke, Roger Tyack, Ross Oliver Collins, Rowan Smith, Rob Matthews, Sandra Backway, Sandra Pritchard, Sara Louise Lobb, Sara Penny, Sharon Edwards, Sharon Marie Burrell, Sharon Rush, Simon Lethane, Simone Marjelam, Stan Spry, Steve Beazely, Steve Jeffers, Steve Northcott, Stuart Thorn, Sue Alvey, Sue Dent, Sue Kinver, Sue Nicholas, Sue Vanstone, Susan Coney, Suzanne Jane Lawrence, Tamsin Dower, Terry Higman, Tom Murt, Tony Allen, Tony Brooks, Tony Clarke, Tony Johnson, Tony Pawlyn, Tracey Dawson, Tracy Childs, Trev Lawrence, Trudie Pearce, Victoria White, Vivien Bottrell, Weni Tarling, and William John Walton. If I have omitted anyone, please accept my sincere apologies and keep up the good work everyone.

Above: A well posed photograph of two boys outside of Pudners Cottage in Poughill, taken by prolific Bude photographer Harry Thorn, the first Thorn photographer in the Thorn photographic dynasty. Harry took this photo in about 1866.[1]

Below: A charming very late Victorian street scene of Stratton. The distinctive tower of St Andrews' parish church can be seen over the roofs of the houses in Townsend at the top of Maiden Street. It appears that the local horse-drawn bus was packed to the gunwales.

Above: A CdV of two fishermen surveying the conditions, while looking out over the breakwater at Bude—a study produced by local photographer Harry Thorn in the early 1860s.

Below: It is 1870, and seventeen-year-old Samuel Thorn poses for his father, the local photographer Harry Thorn, who took this photo, which he produced commercially as a CdV. This view is looking from the breakwater upriver towards Bude; sailing vessels are moored up outside the canal but inside of the breakwater's protective embrace.[2]

Above: A Thorn full-plate albumen print of Bude from Efford Down taken in about 1890. The canal can be seen on the far right with the little iron bridge outside of it. Sir Goldsworthy Gurney's famous castle built on sand can be seen in the dunes with Nanny Moore's Bridge just to its left.

Below: This image is scanned from a Harry Thorn CdV taken in the 1860s; we are looking at the gable of East Cottage across the Bude estuary towards the town.[3]

These two photographs are of the Bude Canal; they are both taken by Harry Thorn. In both photographs, the tub boats are evident; these tub boats were used to transport the mineral-rich sand to the neighbouring fields and along the 35-mile-long Bude Canal for dispersal.[4] The top photo is from a CdV of the late 1860s and the bottom photo is an albumen print that dates from 1875.[5] Note the railway tracks running off of the canal down onto the beach. In the background at the mouth of the estuary can be seen the Bude breakwater.

Above: One half of a stereoview, this photograph was taken by Bude pioneer photographer Harry Thorn. This marvellous image again has an older Samuel Thorn far right of picture; here we are looking along the river towards Bude. Dating evidence provided by the buildings can pinpoint the date to between 1868 and 1870.[6]

Below; A beautiful full-plate albumen print of Nanny Moore's Bridge taken by Harry Thorn in about 1867. On the bridge can be seen Samuel Thorn in his natty hat, looking past him out into the Haven towards the breakwater.[7]

Above: These next two photographs of shipwrecks were produced as CdVs and are important from an academic standpoint as they illustrate how Harry Thorn has enhanced the negative with artistic work to make the scene appear more dramatic than the original negative portrayed. This photograph is of the wreck of the *Georgina*, 25 October 1865; it is interesting as it shows the brave locals forming a human chain to save the drowning sailors from the breaking waves.[8]

Below: Again the original image has been tampered with; this was done by photographer Harry Thorn painting on the glass negative. This wreck is the *Avonmore;* she was lost at Morewenstow on 14 September 1869 with the tragic loss of seven lives.[9]

Above: A CdV of Widemouth Bay by Harry Thorn taken in the 1860s. A lady can be seen in her full-length dress on the cliff edge and a member of the Thorn family, probably Samuel, is leaning on his cane while admiring the view. Salthouse, the cottage in the background, looks a bit ramshackle—a very desolate scene.[10] It is of academic interest as the cottage later became a refreshment house and the road moved back away from the retreating cliff.

Below: On the Cornish Victorian Barton Farm, many daily tasks had to be undertaken by the farm labourers. The images are from Treworgie Barton Farm near St Gennys and show the daily drudgery undertaken as part of the long and busy working day. This photograph shows three farm hands marking a pig: one holds a rope on the pig's snout taught while another is pulling the tail, allowing a third to mark the body of the pig with a distinctive identifying dye.

Above: On the Victorian farm, the horse was king, being used for all the transportation, ploughing, and heavy work, unless the farm had oxen (as was often the custom in Cornwall, they were used for ploughing and pulling wheeled vehicles). Like the horses, oxen were given and responded to individual names. Horses had to be looked after as an expensive and necessary commodity. This meant that horses were well cared for. Here we see the farm worker in the saddlery at the wooden feed bin, measuring out the feed for the horses. The farm hand seen here can also be seen in the manure shed image and wood-cutting photos.

Below: In the manure shed. Here the chemicals were thoroughly mixed and bagged up ready for spreading on the fields. The manure would have been weighed into sacks; the scales can be seen in the background. It was then stored in the manure shed until needed. Note the besom broom laying on the floor in the foreground.

Above: Back-breaking work. The two farm hands that are in the previous photo are using a two-handled saw to cut up a fallen tree. Life was very physical for the Victorian farm hand. The worker on the right is no spring chicken; life was certainly hard.

Below: This is a full-plate albumen print taken looking down Lower St Stephen's Hill towards the castle, which can be seen perched on the hill in the distance; this photograph, taken by Henry Hayman (the prolific Launceston photographer), definitely predates the 1878 renovation of the castle although this pin-sharp image is later than 1870, when the Methodist Chapel was built; its spire can be seen in the photo.

Above: This photograph of Southgate Launceston was taken after the alterations had been made by the Historical Society in the early 1860s; prior to that, the window was a slit window and the building was used as a prison. This photo dates from the late 1860s and was taken by Henry Hayman of Launceston as it proudly pronounces on the bottom of the cabinet card.[11]

Opposite: In 1878, Launceston Castle was in a very poor state of repair and underwent a period of extensive renovations. This large-format mounted photograph was taken during these renovations and shows the rail tracks for the carts to carry the stones up the incline to the masons. Behind the men, a massive stone is being transported on the track on its way up to the masons. Apparently, this large stone was to replace a cracked flagstone and it was the second time it had been attempted to get it up to the castle; according to a contemporary newspaper report, on the first occasion, it fell through the neighbouring Wesleyan Chapel and ended up in their boiler room. The man on the left with the beard is Tom 'Mott' Bennett.

Above left: A CdV taken by Launceston photographer Henry Hayman, it shows the Prisoners' Gate, Launceston Castle during the 1860s. The jail was known as 'Doomsdale'.

Above right: Half of a stereoview and also produced as a CdV, this image shows the Western Gate of Launceston Castle taken in the 1850s by Henry Hayman. The ghostly figure on the right-hand side was caused by the lady moving during the fifteen-second exposure time; these were still very early days and photographic plates of this era were very slow to react to the light.

Opposite above: A full-plate albumen print of Southgate, Launceston, after the crenulations had been added on top of the building to celebrate Queen Victoria's Golden Jubilee, which took place in 1887. Judging by the cleanliness of the stone work, this photo would probably have been taken shortly after the alterations.

Opposite below: Henry Hayman produced this albumen print of St Mary Magdalene parish church, Launceston, in the 1860s. This church, one of the finest in Britain, was built in 1511 by Henry Trecarrell and is famed for its magnificent granite exterior.

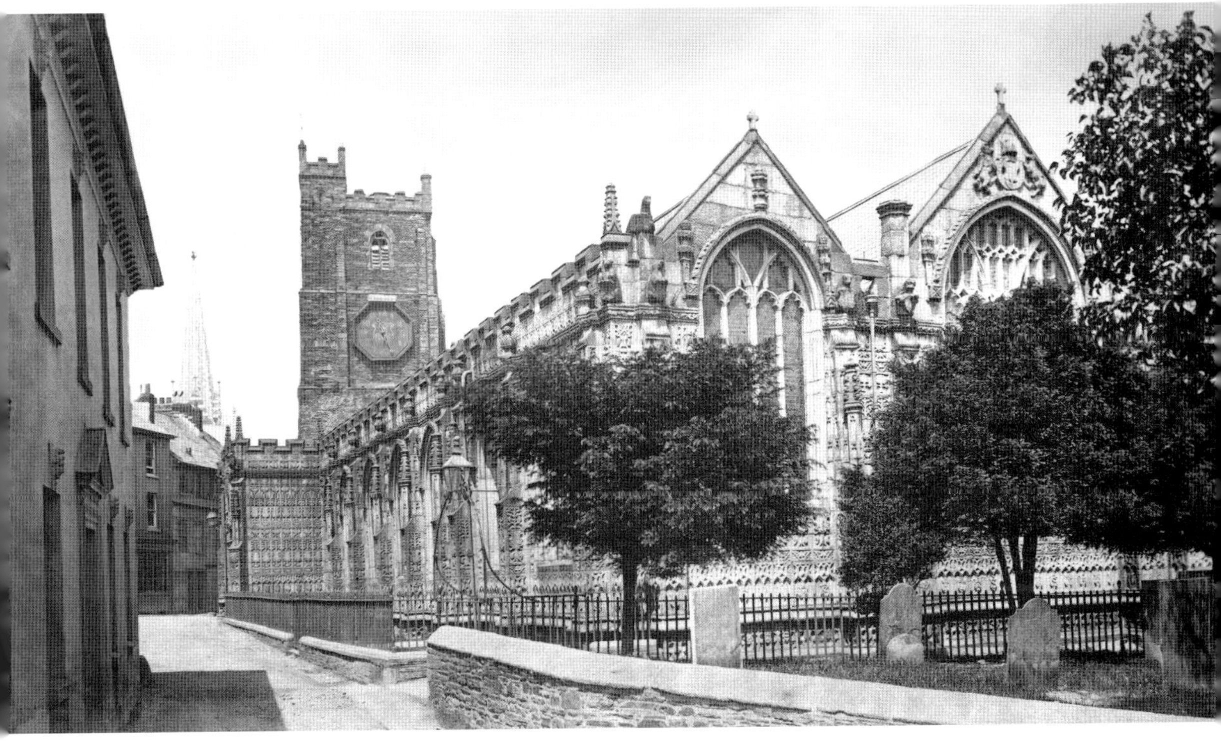

Above: Launceston Grammar School pupils are photographed alongside their masters, *c*. 1871. The master in the back row on the far left is the Reverend Samuel Childs-Clarke, BA MA, who was born in 1821. He was vicar of St Thomas by Launceston and also headmaster of the Grammar School; to his left is Mr Priest. The master on the far right is Mr Bosworthick.

Among the boys from the left to right back row were A. Nicholls, W. Eggins, S. Onslow, W. Folkes-Thompson (who was to become a doctor and mayor of the borough), F. Proctor, F. Lewis, F. Gubbin, Parnell, J. Powell, R. Coad, K. Daunt, F. Gubbin, A. Daunt, A. H. Grigg, Jenkin, C. Clarke, W. Shearm, G. Clarke, Couch, W. Clarke, M. Derry, Alg. Nicholls, Onslow, W. Geake, Bell, T. Martin, W. Gubbin, Vivian, G. White, H. Gubbin, White, and others. Luckily, the names of the people on this CdV were recorded in a local magazine back in the 1920s.

Below: Northcott Mouth Cottage, an albumen print taken in the very early 1870s. Samuel Thorn, the photographer's son, is talking to the cottage residents John and Mary Curtis. Northcott is a hamlet not far to the south of Bude.[12]

An albumen print taken in about 1870 of the ketch *Thomasine and Mary* after she was changed from sloop to ketch rig; she was built in Boscastle in 1855 by T. R. Avery and photographed as she was lowering her sails after entering Boscastle harbour. She is moored just inside the harbour. The small vessels in the foreground are called hobblers; they were used to assist coastal trading vessels, to manoeuvre and tow them when assistance was required.

Above: This full-plate albumen photograph of Boscastle harbour was taken by Harry Thorn before 1876 (probably as early as the 1860s). The 10-inch bore hawsers or junks as they were called are laid doubled up along the sixteenth-century quay wall, interwoven around the bollards; they were used on the larger vessels to protect against the heavy groundswells on the treacherous north coast. Massive tree trunks and branches are stored on the quay beside a moored-up trading smack; these would have been felled in the Valency Valley and are awaiting transportation to the shipbuilding ports of Padstow or Appledore where these eagerly sought curved logs would be used as frames or knees. The little sloop-rigged smack *Bottreaux Castle* was built in 1844 at Padstow just around the coast. Her combings are open to allow access from the deck for her punt, which is alongside her. She was wrecked at Boscastle in 1879 on entering the harbour.

Left: This beautiful photo of the *Alpha* looking back towards the entrance to Boscastle harbour was taken in 1898 by James Moody Cooke. He was one of the first press photographers in London and, at one time, part-owner of this ketch along with his partners, the Slade family of Appledore.

Above: This image looking up the Valency Valley is one of the earliest known photographs of Boscastle, taken in the late 1860s and produced as an albumen print by Launceston photographer Henry Hayman. The waterwheel of the mill can be seen behind the roof of the white cottage on the left. The white building in the centre of the photo is Scott's Wellington Hotel.[13]

Below: Fore Street, Boscastle, photographed by Henry Hayman of Launceston, looking up the hill towards the site of the twelfth-century motte-and-bailey castle, past Granny Cobbledick's sweet shop, Tinker's Cottage, and Smuggler's Cottage. This area around the site of the original Bottreaux Castle has the quaintest cottages in the village. Above the roofs can be see the bell tower of the school, dating the photo to no earlier than the mid-1870s.

Above: Trevillett Mill, Bossiney, captured in a stereoview taken during the 1850s. Outside the mill are standing the miller and his family. This little gem is one of the earliest photographs in this book. The building, now much extended, still stands to this day and is now a high-end holiday cottage.

Below: This small photograph of Tintagel Vicarage would have been taken in the 1870s. This building has long gone and was at the top of the hill leading to St Materiana's church, looking towards the main street. St Materiana's church is the parish church of Tintagel and is situated on the cliffs between Trevena and Tintagel Castle.

Above: This CdV of Tintagel Castle dating from the very early 1860s was taken by Harry Thorn of Bude. It is looking from the cliff down and across the cove towards Merlin's Cave, which lies below the remains of the castle perched on top of the cliffs at Tintagel Haven. On the left of the photo is the winch with a windlass situated on raised stone platforms; this was used for raising cargo and small craft from the beach below. Note the rubber stamp used to apply Harry Thorn's details to the right-hand edge of the card.

Below: A full plate albumen print by Harry Thorn, *c.* 1865, bearing the Thorn blind stamp. It shows activities taking place on the beach below Tintagel Castle; what looks like an uninteresting scene is actually fascinating. A smack, probably the *Bee*, is beached in Tintagel Haven and is being discharged onto temporary rails using a wagon.[14] The two pairs of rails lead out across the sand to below the winch used to raise cargo up the cliff. On the walkway are horses, one with a loaded cart, and two men stood in the background; young Samuel Thorn is leaning on the rowing boat watching the busy scene. Running down the valley and over Merlin's Cave is a pipe that runs from the top of the hill above the path, under the path down the valley, and over Merlin's Cave, where there is a footbridge alongside it; the rocks are supported by pit props and the cliff has been excavated since the earlier image was taken: this is Wheal Heart, a silver and lead mine to the right of Merlin's Cave. The winch and A-frame had a windlass or whim on raised platforms powered by a horse or donkey.

Above: Another CdV taken in the 1860s showing the castle remains. Tintagel Castle was a very popular tourist destination in Victorian times, so early images of it are reasonably common. Harry Thorn obviously found it worth his while making the trip from Bude to photograph the ruins, which would probably have been stocked locally in the Tintagel shops and surrounding area.

Below: Fore Street Tintagel in the late 1870s or early 1880s, before the building now known as the Old Post Office had a wall built around the garden. A buggy is outside the front of the house. The photographer is unknown; this image was taken from the original glass full-plate negative.

Above: Built in the fourteenth century, this famous Cornish longhouse was photographed and recorded for posterity on this albumen print taken by Henry Hayman of Launceston in the early 1860s. With its undulating roof, the building is full of character—a photographer's dream. The house right in the centre of Tintagel is now known as the Old Post Office and is currently owned by the National Trust, who opens it to the public.

Below: The following series of four photographs of the Old Delabole Slate Company quarry were taken in the late 1870s or early 1880s. At first glance, they do not look very interesting, but on closer inspection, they are very interesting and rare images. This one is looking west across Grove Quarry towards Delabole village. Above the quarry can be seen some of the slate works and the house of the commercial manager of the quarry; at this time, it would have been Job Hockaday and family. The house was demolished in the 1930s due to rat infestation. If you look very closely, various working machinery can be seen in the bottom of the quarry.

Looking south-west across the Old Delabole Slate Company's Grove Quarry. At the bottom of the incline can be seen twin rail tracks and parts of a vertical drainage system that was worked and driven by the Cornish pump engines, which can be seen on the quarry cliff top.

Another view of Old Delabole Slate Company's quarry looking south towards the west face haulage incline on the right, and at the main incline to the pit, bottom left. It is amazing to look at these photos and see the ingenuity and engineering skills required to work this quarry profitably in the late nineteenth century.

Above: A late nineteenth-century full-plate albumen produced by commercial photographers Valentine, looking back into the heart of the town of Camelford from the garden of the Manor House. By the time this photo was taken, Valentine and Francis Frith had photographers working all over the globe aimed at the profitable tourist market; their images provide an invaluable record for historians.

Below: Port Isaac, looking down onto the harbour and Platt. This charming full-plate albumen was produced by Valentine probably in the early 1890s. The luggers have been pulled up the beach and onto the Platt away from the incoming tide.

How smart this group of nurses look, captured on a cabinet card by Bodmin photographer A. Bond. With the County Lunatic Asylum being in Bodmin, there would have been a lot of nurses living in the area.

A charming photograph showing Charles Bennett's derelict tailor's shop. It was situated in Fore Street, Bodmin. He was out of business by 1889 and the neighbouring shop, Sleeman bakers, is first recorded also in 1889 so it is likely this atmospheric photo was taken in the very early 1890s.

A pin-sharp albumen print of a Tudor house that stood in Pool Street, Bodmin.The house was pulled down in 1889. It was known as the Porch House for obvious reasons; it certainly was an imposing building, and with hindsight would have been a wonderful house to preserve for future generations to enjoy.

This CdV is by Bodmin photographer W. W. Oke, who was working in the 1870s and died in the late 1880s.[15] This studio study is of a pair of street urchins studio posed and taken in the late 1870s; it looks like the boys are captured eagerly sharing a pasty.

Bodmin locals crowd onto Mount Folly to celebrate Queen Victoria's Golden Jubilee in 1887. According to contemporary newspaper accounts, after a procession from Mount Folly to the church, followed by a service, the parade marched to the top of the Beacon led by the 3rd Battalion Duke of Cornwall's Light Infantry (DCLI) Band. Afterwards, a tea was held for 2,000 people at the Market House and outside the Mayor's House; the celebrations ended with illuminations and a bonfire on the Beacon.

This image was taken in the late 1850s and is half of a stereoview. It was taken by professional photographer Richard Yeo of Plymouth. He had taken the long trip down to photograph the Long Gallery in Lanhydrock House near Bodmin, which was still owned by the Robartes family at the time this image was taken. The house is now in the ownership of the National Trust and is open to the public.

Above: A late Victorian mounted albumen photo of Dennison Road, Bodmin. The ramshackle cottages on the left were demolished for the road widening scheme. The photographer was standing on the junction of Higher Bore Street and Lower Bore Street, looking down Dennison Road towards Cardell Street.

Below: Bodmin Police station and courts when first built in 1867, captured on a CdV by Wadebridge photographer C. R. Lobb. The police station was in use until 1973.

Above: Tredethy House is a small manor house dating from the seventeenth century in the rural parish of St Mabyn. The house underwent heavy restoration under the supervision of Cornish architect Silvanus Trevail in 1892. The house after Trevail's renovations looked very different from the pre-1892 property. This series of full-plate albumen photographs have arched tops similar to stereoviews of the 1860s—a fashion of this time that suggests a possible date for the images. This distant view of the house shows its symmetrical design with glass houses extending on each side.

Below: This series of photographs of Tredethy is included in its entirety, with the exception of a general view across the valley and an image of the rockery. These are an important series of photographs, as they document a small Cornish estate in the middle of the nineteenth century. This image features one of the glass houses and Tredethy House from the other side, clearly showing the double gable ends.

Above: The Tredethy stable block. A very imposing ivy-clad building, it has the appearance of a well-built house with odd but attractively shaped tiles. The entrance to the hayloft appears to be in the centre of the building and I wonder if the other upper floor windows were staff accommodation.

Below: Tredethy House's Gardener's Cottage. This building appears to be a very well-built and sturdy property. Note the ornate ridge tiles, heavy granite lintels over the downstairs windows, and unusual central opening panes to the windows. The three members of staff, standing posed for the photograph, are all also in the staff photo included later in the book.

Above: Tredethy farm house—another well-built property with apparently no expense spared, heavy carved granite lintels, and central opening windows. The staff outside pose for the photo, probably the first time they had ever seen a camera.

Below: The Vinery at Tredethy House—a long and impressive Victorian glass house. This building was put aside solely for the cultivation of grapes. To the left behind the Vinery can be seen the distinctive stable block.

Above: Inside the Vinery; the vines have been trailed up the inside side wall of building and trained down the wooden frame of the building so the bunches of grapes would hang down as can clearly be seen in this photograph, this image would have been technically very difficult in those early days of photography.

Below: Tredethy staff. We have seen most of these characters in previous photographs; I would presume the gentleman in the centre with a cockerel on his lap is the head man as he has been in most of the images.

Two rare late Victorian mounted photographs of Wheelwrights in Wadebridge. In the bottom photograph, on the door behind them are certificates from competitions; presumably, they were well-skilled men. The men worked for W. A. Hawkey, whose business was situated by the river in Egloshayle Road. The business was described in *Kelly's Directories* of 1889, 1893, and 1897 as carriage builders, wheelwrights, and steam saw mills; by 1902, with the birth of the automobile, they are described as cycle agents, carriage builders, and wheelwrights—Hawkey was obviously evolving with the times. In the top photo leaning against the spokes is Dick Eyers. The three men sat in the front row are Mr Hooper from Ball, Bill Hawkey, and Tommy Mitchell; Mr Hawkey, who was the proprietor, is the man with the beard. In the bottom photo with the moustache and bowler on is Hugh Salmon and on the opposite end of the row with the beard is Richard Salmon.

Above: Two police constables and most of the village have turned out for this photograph taken beside the parish church of St Issey in 1869. Sadly, the tower was hit by lightning and almost totally collapsed as can be seen in this photograph taken by John Reynolds of Padstow and produced as a CdV. The church tower was not rebuilt until 1871.

Below: A cart makes its way off Little Petherick Bridge up the hill to Padstow, past Church Cottages on its right. It rarely snows in these parts, but there is certainly snow on the ground so it was possibly taken through the harsh winter of 1891, when there was a famous blizzard. This cabinet card of a rarely photographed village was produced by an unknown photographer.

Navvies work on the completion of the bridge over Little Petherick Creek and the track into Padstow. These two photographs were taken by F. E. Box probably in 1898; the line to Padstow was opened in 1899.[16]

Above: The first train into Padstow on 23 March 1899. It was taken by St Merryn photographer Alex Old. The crowds throng around the newly arrived train; a welcoming party of local dignitaries were waiting on the newly built station platform for the grand arrival. It was a huge day for the town as the railway was to bring the tourists in, and export fish from the visiting fishing fleets over the next few decades. These excited locals could have had no idea that in fewer than seventy years, the line and station would be closed as part of Dr Richard Beeching's cuts. To build the station and approaches, the Higher Yard, a thriving shipyard with a dry dock and a multitude of associated buildings, had to be levelled and the dock filled in, with the dry dock wall becoming the retaining wall for the infill making the present-day station land.[17]

Below: This is a large-format albumen photo of the Customs House, Riverside, Padstow, *c*. 1860.[18] The customs gig would have been used to get the customs officers to vessels waiting at anchor in the River Camel and is seen hanging on davits ready for action. The present-day building has a conservatory on the front where the gig is seen hanging. When the photo was taken, the gig would be lowered straight into the water, where today there is a road. With the coming of the railway, much land along Riverside was reclaimed, a road was put in, and a dock made with train tracks going past this building to the Inner Quay. Amazingly, this building is now about 50 yards from the water with a road and the Padstow harbour commissioner's car park and offices on reclaimed land.

Above: This amazing photo was taken after the school tower was built in 1875 and is just visible on the tree line. This scene, which would be unrecognisable to most people, is a view of Padstow from the north looking back across the harbour with the Higher Yard in the distance; a wooden ship can be seen being built on stocks in the yard. The long building next to the shipyard was the old Drill Hall; to its right is Court House with its overhanging window overlooking the estuary with a slipway below it. Court House was later shortened when the road was put along Riverside. To the right of the sail can be seen the warehouse building now part of the Old Customs House Hotel. The entire foreshore to the left has since been reclaimed with the coming of the railway and building of the road and dock.[19]

Below: A difficult CdV to make out, it is very early and shows Riverside at Padstow before it was reclaimed from the river; the Drill Hall, which can be seen in the previous photo, had not been built when this photo was taken in the 1860s. The warehouse building that is the present-day Old Customs House Hotel now dominating the corner of Riverside and South Quay would not be built for another twenty years, its site at this time being covered with fishermen's cottages.[20, 21]

Above: A similar but later view to the previous image, this albumen print by Valentine was probably taken in the 1890s. I have included it as a good comparison to the series of CdVs working around the quay. It is a lovely view looking down on the wet dock of the shipyard, which had gates to keep the water out if necessary. The Customs House gig is on the walkway outside the building and a low boathouse has been built. The warehouse building is now on the corner of Riverside on the site of the cottages, only one of the fishermen's cottages remains at this time.

Below: A CdV of South Quay Padstow, taken from on board a vessel. The fishermen's cottages are to the left and to their right is the Caledonia Inn. The shop on the front belonged to Robert Grigg, who had by this time moved from his Duke Street premises. The steamer in the photo is the paddle steam tug *Amazon*; she was registered in Padstow in 1872, and this would be an appropriate date for the photo.[22]

Above: A cropped portion of a CdV from the 1870s showing the house on the Strand with a rounded front; this has a courtyard in the centre and was once the Shambles or Market House. It is where, in ancient times, meat would have been sold. I have seen the old hooks in the beams where the meat would have been hung for sale. The slipway is known locally as Obby Oss Slip as the 'oss' would go down and drink from the quay on mayday.

Below: This CdV is of a similar date to the previous image and shows a broad overview of the town. Over the quay in the background can be seen New Street, leading up the hill to Malt House Corner; the malt house with its huge sliding doors can clearly be seen with its associated cottages carrying on up the hill. In the foreground is South Quay. On the far left are fishermen's cottages juxtaposed with the Caledonia Inn, which was located at the bottom of Strand Street. Continuing along South Quay, we have a run of four-storey buildings giving it an industrial feel. To the right is a triangular area known as the Drang, which seems to be full of rubble; behind the Drang, the ground floor of the buildings seems to be open to the elements and supported by pillars, indicative of pilchard curing sheds.[23] As we move farther right, we can see more fishermen's cottages on Market Strand.

Above: In this CdV, we again see the clinker-built wooden steam paddle tug *Amazon*, built in 1856 in Gateshead. She weighed 12 tons, was 72 feet long, and drew 7 feet; a large vessel powered by a 20-hp single cylinder engine, she was kept busy towing the sailing vessels in and out of the tricky to navigate Camel Estuary. She is seen here moored against the Strand; behind her is a tall circular structure, which appears to have a chimney, this structure remains a mystery. The photograph was probably taken by local photographer John Reynolds on the *Amazon*'s arrival in Padstow during 1872.

Opposite: This wonderful CdV taken on the North Quay Padstow in the 1860s obviously caused a great crowd to form at the sight of the unfamiliar camera. The building that seems to have been a hardware store at this time is now the Shipwrights Inn.[24] This photo has always been referred to as 'the sawpit', referring to the sawpit used to cut the timber for the shipyard, but I can find no evidence for this either in the photo or the tithe map of the 1840s.

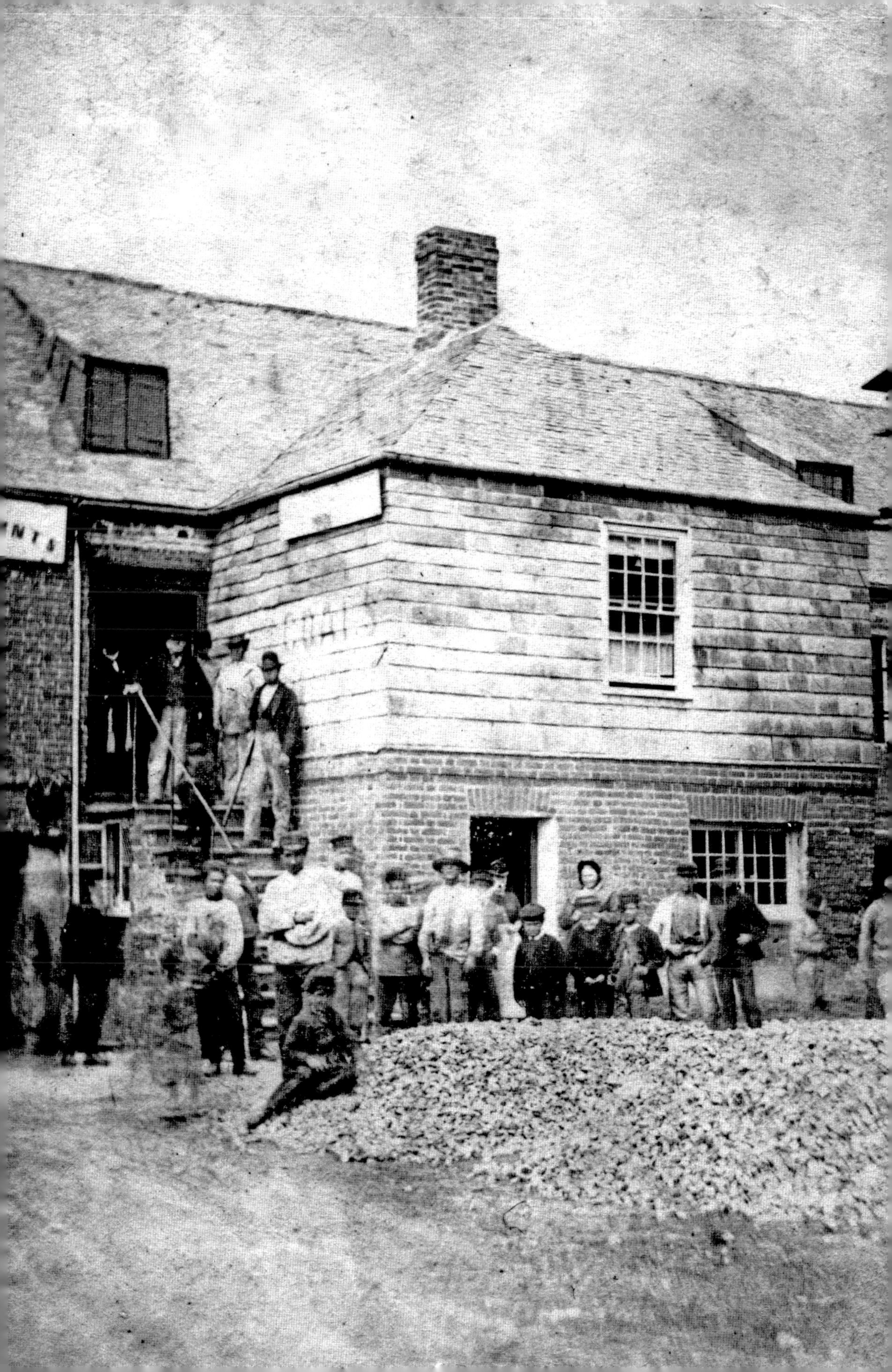

Above: What an incredible photograph of the Lower Beach Padstow in the 1860s. Shipwrights work on three boats on the beach adjacent to the Lower Yard, which had its own small harbour walls and slipway, making the beach ideal for ships to moor and be worked on. In the days of wooden sailing ships, Padstow was famed for its shipyards and her vessels were in high demand. The Red Brick building which was built *c.* 1870 was later altered to have a distinctive mansard roof which dominated the North Quay for over 100 years. When this photograph was taken presumably by Padstow photographer John Reynolds the building still had the old roof line.[25]

Below: The Lower Yard Padstow also locally known as Cowls Yard after Mr Cowl, who owned and ran it at the end of the nineteenth century. It was the last local working shipyard of the wooden ship era, this photo taken in the 1890s. Work is being carried out on the ketch, but the yard was no longer building new large sailing vessels from scratch with the last one being launched from the Port from this yard in 1887. Later, this yard was taken on by Mr Brabyn, who again built vessels, but moving with the times, he concentrated on smaller vessels. Now the building has been demolished and flats built in its place, though its original harbour walls and slipway survive.

Above: A CdV from the 1870s looking over Padstow, with Hicks and Hawken's drapers shop in Broad Street centre of picture; they are listed in *Kelly's Directory* of 1873. In the next photo, Hicks's shop is shown before Hawken was a partner and the frontage of the shop protruded onto the pavement; in this photo, the shop front is as it is today. This image predates Tredwen Court in Middle Street, which was built in 1875. At the top of the photo can be seen an ink number, below that is a curious building with windows all around standing on pillars; this was apparently a summer house that overlooked the town and estuary.

Below: A Cabinet card taken before 1873 of Broad Street, Padstow, looking up Llanadwell Street; the shop on the left with the interesting windows was the Evan Griffith chemist shop. Straight ahead was Sleeman's Ironmongers, which had been trading for a long time as it is listed in the first *Kelly's Directory* of 1856. Hicks drapers are distinctive with the boarding over the windows; these windows protrude out over the present-day pavement. The photographer obviously asked the locals to keep still and look at the camera for the photograph.

Above: An albumen print of the market in Padstow—what a bustling scene, which was captured after the Padstow Institute was built in 1883. Evan Griffith chemist's shop is still on the corner of Broad Street. It is interesting to see the window of the drapers covered with calico, protecting the display from the sun. In the background can be seen the post office where the Market meets Duke Street.[26]

Below: This is a mysterious image as it is an ambrotype, suggesting it dates from the 1850s but it depicts William Brown the postmaster, outside his post office in Duke Street, Padstow. The post office sign can clearly be seen on the window. It is a mystery as according to *Kelly's Directory*, the post office was in Church Street right up to 1883; all I can assume is that Mr Brown did not inform *Kelly's Directory* when he moved as I cannot imagine this form of photography being used this late.

Above: St Edmunds House, Padstow, captured on a mounted albumen print taken in the 1870s; the Rawlings family, who were local gentry and merchants having several large properties in the town, are seen tending the garden of their house. The house was used by previous generations of their family as a court house.[27]

Below: Padstow had several private schools dotted around the town. The Paynter family gave the plot of land on the outskirts of the town for the new board school to be built. In this full-plate mounted albumen print, we can see the newly completed buildings and gardens in 1875. There were separate schools for boys and girls and the left-hand wing of the building was the headmaster's house. This was built before the main road came down past the school as the fancy-shaped wall and railings had to be set back toward the school and made into a straight run. The school has now been relocated up the hill and these buildings and others built in the grounds have now been converted into private houses.

Above: Padstow is famous for its ancient custom of the Padstow Obby Oss. This photograph taken in about 1897 is probably the earliest known photograph of the event. Taken in the hamlet of Treator just over a mile from the town, the oss would make the annual trip to drink from Treator Pool. The oss is made from sailcloth or canvas and was then tarred or painted. The canvas was fitted over an oak hoop; this gave it the distinctive oval shape. The snappers were worked by the carrier from inside by means of a rope. This crystal sharp image, which was widely reproduced as a postcard, is from a full-plate albumen print by the marvellous St Merryn photographer Alex Old.

Opposite: Another early photograph of the obby oss, this one was presented as a cabinet card and taken by A. J. F. Bond of Bodmin. It is beautifully composed on the steps of Abbey House, Padstow's late fifteenth-century guildhall situated on the North Quay.

Above: In 1858, an act of Parliament was passed and issued as a booklet: *Improvements to the River Camel*. One of the improvements was to remove the bluff of Stepper Point. Stepper Point is the western most headland on the entrance to the River Camel. The sailing vessels using the busy port of Padstow were regularly coming to grief on the Doom Bar due to losing the wind in the lee of Stepper Point; this was compounded by the strong Bristol Channel tides and treacherous sandbars forming the Narrows which ran beside Stepper Point and was the only channel into Padstow harbour. Removing the bluff allowed sailing vessels to catch the wind for longer to reach a safe anchorage and wait for the flood tide to make her way to port. This photo shows the men toiling away at removing the bluff in 1859; one can be seen high up on the cliff wielding a pick, while another two are working at filling a metal wheeled skip; it is obvious from the photo that work is well underway.

Below: The *Pioneer* was a stage coach that in Victorian times ran between Padstow, St Columb, Wadebridge, and Boscastle. Pulled by a team of four horses, this stage coach looks pretty full; while some sat cosily in the warm, the other more unfortunate passengers were well wrapped up outside. Note the ladder slung across the back to provide the passengers on the top easier access.

Above: John Reynolds of Padstow, photographer and watchmaker produced this CdV, which dates from the late 1860s. Although in *Views and Likenesses* Professor Charles Thomas suggests Reynolds was working from 1873, I have contemporary dated CdVs by him from as early as 1862.[28] This view shows St Michael's church, Porthilly, near Rock on the banks of the Camel Estuary with a pair of well-dressed ladies in the churchyard.

Below: Another CdV by Padstow photographer John Reynolds dating from the late 1860s. This view is of St Enodoc church in the parish of St Minver, the church is famous for being completely buried by windblown sea sand, when buried entry was gained through the roof using a ladder. In the background across the Camel Estuary can be seen Stepper Point after the bluff had been cut back during the late 1850s and early 1860s.

Above: A Victorian Cornish farmhouse: Gluvian Farm near St Columb. This photograph taken in 1883 illustrates the growth and expansion of the farm. The old thatched farmhouse forms a wing behind the later sturdy stone-built and tiled front of the house. In the background can be seen the ramshackle old thatched farm labourer's cottages with cob walls. There are holes in the roof and the buildings look derelict. The ladies of the house are out in the front garden and a cow and boy are in the moway.

Below: The board of guardians for the St Columb Work House, locally known as The Retreat after the name was changed in 1933 when its role changed to a home for the mentally ill. This very large cabinet photograph is taken outside of the entrance in the 1880s. The board would have been made up from specific numbers of people from each parish in the ward as set out and amended after the formation of the St Columb Poor Law Union of 9 May 1837.

Sampson Liddicoat, photographer of St Columb, captured Queen Victoria's Diamond Jubilee celebrations in 1897 in this fantastic mounted albumen print. It is taken looking down Fore Street at the elaborate arch and platform, below can be seen Major Cardell and the volunteers who led the parade. The town was decked out in flowers with arches of greenery. In the morning, there was a parade from the Fair Field led by the band of the volunteers and 500 children from the Board School to the church, where a service was held. After the service was a tea in Union Square and the Market. Next it was time for sports, which were attended by an astounding 2,000 people; after the sports, there was a dance and carnival. This was followed by an illumination of houses and a torchlight parade with some people wearing fancy dress paraded up to Castle an Dinas where a bonfire was lit; a fireworks display completed a long and full day.

Above: St Mawgan village. The shop on the left is listed in *Kelly's Directory* of 1883 as Joseph Germans, grocer, draper, and post office; his name can be seen on the glass above the door. The landlord of the neighbouring sixteenth-century Falcon Inn is shown as Samuel Gilbert in the same directory. According to the Falcon Inn's own excellent website, the building has been an inn since 1758 but only called the Falcon since the 1880s, the name being changed by landlord Samuel Gilbert who took over the pub from his sister Mary, in 1839. This image is taken from an unattributed original full-plate glass negative.

Opposite page: A late Victorian pair of photographs of St Mawgan Village. They are taken from the ford across the River Menathyl, which runs through the village. The top photograph is titled 'the school' and shows two men by a buggy, the old school building behind them to our left. The bottom photo is a general view looking back up the village.

Above: During the sixth century, Welsh Missionary Meugan or Mawgan landed at Mawgan Porth, just down the valley from Mawgan village. He settled and formed a monastery that later became the Manor of Lanherne, named after the area which is called the Vale of Lanherne. The monastery was dissolved in the eleventh century, becoming a manor house for the Arundell family and it becomes their main residence from the fourteenth century. In 1794, this fine house was given to the nuns of the Carmelites as a convent. This photograph shows it in the 1860s and is one half of a stereoview sold by G. S. Drew, bookseller of St Columb.

Below: This beautifully composed photograph is of Lawry's Mill, St Mawgan, taken in the 1890s by commercial photographers Valentine. The photographer has the mill and associated buildings framed by the trees looking across the wooden bridge spanning the River Menathyl. He has carefully scoured the derelict buildings for props and found a broken wagon wheel, ladder, and wooden wheelbarrow complete with mattock to pull the viewer into the foreground.

Above: Dressing the land with calcium-rich sea sand has been a treatment for the local soils since ancient times; it is a practice that continues in these parts to this day. Here we see a late Victorian farm labourer filling his wagon with sea sand at Mawgan Porth; he has nose bags on the horses while they rest before the heavy load requires pulling up the valley to be stockpiled and leached by the rain before being spread on the land.

Below: Three nattily dressed Victorians sit on a pile of logs to pose for a photograph at Tregurrian, a hamlet on the coast road between Padstow and Newquay. These days, we drive the coast road and expect no delays; back when this photo was taken, there were quite a few gates on the road to prevent livestock from straying, the road being just a rough earth track barely suitable for horse drawn buggies. This photo dates from the last years of the nineteenth century.

The Royal Institution of Cornwall held regular excursions for its members; this image was taken on one of their excursions during 1872 to Trevelgue Head on the outskirts of Newquay to examine two barrows, which had recently been excavated by Victorian antiquarian William Copeland Borlase. The top photograph is a full-plate albumen print capturing the party on top of the excavated barrow. The lower photograph is half of a stereoview showing a close up of the capstone of the burial chamber in the barrow with a gentleman poking out of the structure, could this be Mr Borlase?

Above: This CdV by Mitchell of St Austell is a very early image of Newquay. The harbour's central pier had a wooden structure carrying railway lines; it was built in 1872 and is not in this photo. The consensus of opinion is that this was taken in the very late 1860 but it is possible it could date from as early as the late 1850s, yet more research is required to prove this. The harbour is packed with sailing ships. The Treffry Tramroad disappears into the tunnel to the south of the harbour; this horse-worked mineral railway later became Cornwall Mineral Railways.

Below: A similar view to the last image, this albumen print by an unknown photographer bears the date 1883. The wagons for the Mineral Railway are visible in this photograph; the northern most end of the central jetty can just be seen poking out past the cellars. It is interesting to look into the background and see how few houses there were compared to the Newquay of today.

This full-plate albumen taken in 1887 is looking from the west across Newquay harbour onto Towan Beach. Ketches are moored up on the central jetty and the smaller vessels are beached secured to their moorings. The fully laden Mineral Railway wagons can be seen alongside the outer harbour wall.

Newquay harbour in the 1890s. This image is scanned from a full-plate glass negative by an unidentified photographer. Looking north over the harbour and out to sea, we can see a ketch being loaded from a wagon on the central jetty. The plan of the railway tracks along the quay can easily be understood in this image; it is clear to see how the wagons could work alongside any of the quays. Behind the harbour can be seen the old fish cellars.

Loading coal in Newquay harbour. The image is undated but must be right at the cusp of the Edwardian era. The wagon is standing on the outer wall looking west into the harbour. The coal would have come down from Wales. In the background can be seen the wooden supports for the railway tracks to the central jetty.

Beach Road, Newquay, captured in the 1890s and scanned from an unattributed full-plate glass negative. A young Victorian lady reads her book as she sits outside the entrance to Chy-an-Mor on Beach Road. As we look over her shoulder, the road winds down to Towan Beach with Newquay Bay in the distance.

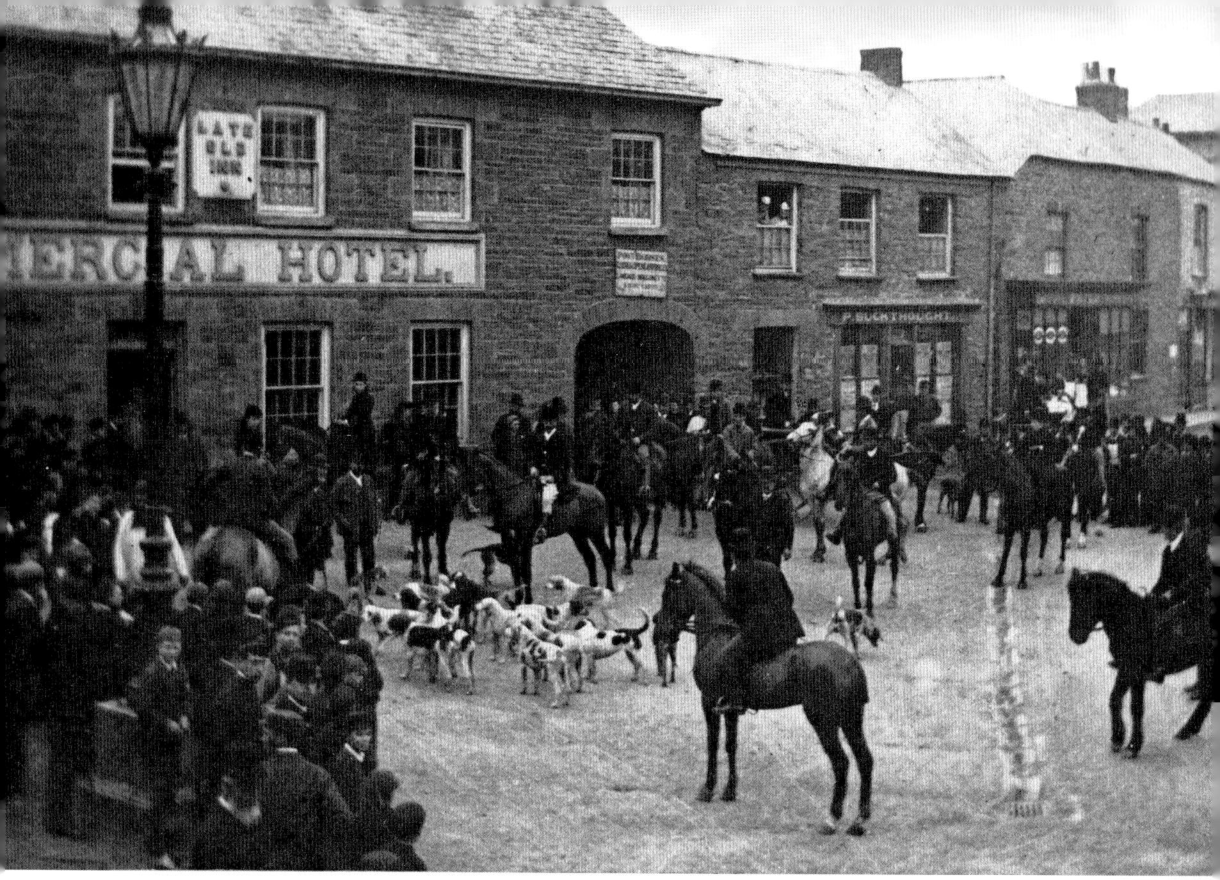

Above: A cabinet card from the 1890s by Wallace Bennetto of Newquay looking at the North Cornwall Hunt as it gathers outside the Commercial Hotel in Fore Street, Newquay. A plaque on the building says formerly the New Inn, though we know the building today as the Central Inn.

Below: A wonderful photo of an unrecognisable Perranporth, captured forever during the early 1850s. The mine workings in the foreground was the engine house of Wheal Leisure, in the distance on the cliffs is Wheal Droskyn Mine. On the far right can be seen Chapel Rock. Looking back to the beach, seine boats are pulled up onto the bar with their associated fish cellars to the right—how time has dramatically changed this town.

Marriott's Shaft and Engine House, South Wheal Francis, Carnkie, St Agnes. This and the following four images are all of the St Agnes District and date from the 1890s. It housed a 75-inch cylinder pumping engine, which was installed in 1847; this engine had a dual purpose as it also pumped the water from Pascoe's Shaft. A Bal Maiden is standing next to the horse, other bal maidens are further right, they were blurred because were busy working beneath the trestle, the bal maidens are wearing their traditional gook and towsers. Their gooks, a form of protective hat, are tied so they cover their mouth and nose suggesting dusty work. The ladies are working with their long-handled shovels spalling the ore; the good ore would be sorted into one pile for the stamps and the poor or discarded waste into another pile to be dumped at the burrows.

Above: Another more distant view of Marriott's Shaft, Wheal Francis—in the background can be seen the pumping engine house and chimney; in the foreground are some of the associated sheds and conveyor trestles used for moving ore, probably housing the water intensive buddles hence the wooden launders leading into the sheds; buddeling was used to separate the fine ore from the gangue which was later disposed of. One point of interest in this photo is the keeve in the cart on the right, being round and high-sided, it would be better suited for containing the ore as it came out of the chute above.

Below: Pascoe's Engine House, South Wheal Francis, Carnkie, St Agnes. This engine house had a slit window, which was not uncommon in this area at this time. Pascoe's Shaft was named after Captain Pascoe who was a mine shareholder and manager; he emigrated to Utah in 1872. Interestingly, the building earlier housed an 80-inch engine, this was the largest ever built in the St Austell Foundry, being completed in 1881 for Old Shepherd's Mine, St Newlyn East, near Newquay. It was bought second-hand for South Wheal Francis in 1887 and started working the same year. The engine cylinder was put in through the large cylindrical door at the back of the engine house; the boiler house is on the left. In the background, a whim engine can be seen; this probably furnished Grenville Shaft, which was to the west.

Above: Thomas's Engine House, Carnkie, St Agnes; Thomas's Shaft was sunk by the important West Wheal Bassett mine in the 1850s. In 1854, it had a 60-inch steam engine erected on it. The greatest period of development on this site was during the 1850s when West Wheal Bassett Mine began sinking Thomas's Shaft. This engine house was unfortunately damaged by fire a few years after this photo was taken. The engine was decommissioned in 1899.

Below: St Agnes harbour in Trevaunance Cove; the road from St Agnes drops steeply to the north-east and Quay Road runs down the valley, which widens and deepens to the north of the cove. Wheal Kitty and Wheal Penhall's Mine lie on a plateau to the east, Wheal Friendly and Polberro Mine stand on the hillside to the west. This photo taken in the early 1890s shows the hoisting contraptions and the copper hutches remaining on the cliff top just north of the open works at Wheal Luna; this apparatus was used to load the ore onto ships lying in the harbour.

A cabinet card from the 1890s of Elizabeth Dunstan. Known as 'Sherdy', she had an argument with her husband who was a miner, and to teach him a lesson, she filled his pasty with broken crockery or sherds—can you imagine his mates' amusement when he bit into his pasty at 'croust time' (when miners had a break to eat their pasties), and the ribbing he must have taken from the other miners? She was a well-known and well-photographed character; here she is seen peddling candles, which she is proudly displaying to the photographer.

How different life was in the 1880s: this CdV taken at Chacewater shows a proud young boy in his smart uniform with his trusty steed. There is some speculation as to whether he is a telegram boy or worked for the railway, but it is a charming photo and illustrates how young boys were when they started their working lives in late Victorian times.

Above: A rural scene at Comford near Redruth in the 1880s. The building behind the signpost is the present-day Fox and Hounds public house. Chacewater can be read on the signpost pointing right. The small cart looks like it is carrying bags of coal, but the large wagon is slightly more of a mystery, having a large piece of industrial-looking piping with either rubble or chopped wood.

Below: A mounted albumen print taken by Opie of Redruth in 1900. Here is a *précis* of a contemporary newspaper report: for many years, the inhabitants of Lanner have been greatly inconvenienced by having to walk great distances for their drinking water. This has now been resolved due to the generosity of the late Miss Maud Pascoe, with the help of her sister, it had been anticipated to cost £70 but the actual costs double that. Prior to the official opening ceremony on Monday, Reverend A. Darnell made a few remarks to a number of interested spectators prior to the ceremonial turning on of the tap performed by Mrs E. B. Beauchamp of Trevince, after an introduction by her husband. Miss May Dunstan the granddaughter of Mr R. Renale caught the first water in a pitcher. Prayers were said for Miss Maud Pascoe and a commemorative photograph of the granite tap in the square was taken by Mr Opie of Redruth; the granite has inscribed on it: 'In Memoriam Maude P. Pascoe A.D. 1900'.

Above: A very early family photograph of Portreath harbour. My great grandfather Johns was coastguard officer at Portreath and must have acquired it then. This image shows the linear heaps of copper ore piled up ready for loading onto the waiting vessels to take it to Swansea for smelting; the vessels coming back from Swansea would bring in coal, which was needed to power the steam engines driving the local mines pumps. This very industrial scene was taken in the 1850s or 1860s but reprinted as a photographic postcard in the early years of the twentieth century.

Below: Tuckingmill Hill, Redruth, captured by local photographer Matthew Row; we know he was working between 1866 and 1876.[29] The trap has William Thomas Illogan written on it; if that is the name of the driver, he must be William Thomas of Carnkie, born in 1832, who worked as a carpenter and grocer. Assuming he is coming up for forty, this would date this CdV to about 1870.

Above: A mounted albumen print taken by James Chenhalls. He was working at West End Redruth from 1865 right through to after 1910.[30] There is no dating evidence in this photo of thrashing at Carvannell Farm near Fourlanes, but the engine is an early tall chimney type dating from the 1870s, but saying that, these engines were used for years; from the way it is mounted, I would suggest it was printed and mounted in the 1890s but it is a typical Victorian Cornish thrashing scene that would relate to anywhere in the Duchy at that time. Looking at the engine chimney, the flange near the boiler was a hinge so the engine could be lowered down under low carriage house doorways or other obstacles; the engine could not move under its own steam and would have to be pulled to where it was working by a team of four horses.

Above: A fantastic photo by an unknown photographer. It is believed to be either the inside of Harvey's No. 3 Shed, Hayle or Holman's foundry in Camborne. This location is not certain, but it is definitely in the locality as it came with a pair of photos of tin streaming at Rosewarne of an identical format. There is a striking similarity to the image in *Views and Likenesses*, which is also unidentified.[32] It is a very rare image of inside a working Cornish Victorian foundry.

Opposite below: A cabinet card taken by James Chenhalls of Redruth, at the time he was working out of his West End Studio. We know this image predates 1880 because it has not yet been marked 'Chenhalls and Sons'.[31] I am afraid I know no more about the sitter although he was obviously a Victorian pigeon fancier; if anyone knows who he is, please drop me an email. Photographs of this type at this time were very expensive; he must have been very proud of his birds to go to such extravagance.

This CdV by John Moody was taken between 1853 and 1868 (probably in the early 1860s). The lady in the image was Gracie Briney. She was born in Gwennap in 1778 and christened Grace Huchins. While very young, she was sent to work in the copper mines in Redruth; here she was apprenticed under Captain A. Treneer and was taught to drive the horse at the whim, which raised the kibble from below grass. The kibble was a large metal bucket that was filled with ore; close attention would have to be paid so it did not reach the surface with too much speed, as the kibble-lander who would be standing on a platform would have to catch the rim of the bucket with a long metal pot hook and swing it in from the mouth of the mine to empty it. This took strength, coordination, and extreme care and was a very hard job as there was no shelter from wind or rain. Gracie became a kibble-lander and is the only woman we know of in Cornwall to have undertaken this arduous task.

This amazing CdV taken by John Beringer of Helston in 1864 must be one of the earliest existing photographs of a member of the Cornwall Constabulary; this force was formed in 1857. PC 116 William Llewelyn Vosper is the sitter. Before joining the force, he was a labourer from St Dominic near Callington. On 21 August 1863, he was appointed as a constable and stationed at Liskeard. On 17 July the following year, he was transferred to Penzance; however, his service records show that on the very same day, he was ordered to pay for a new truncheon and whistle and to move at his own expense to Camborne. I am presuming that while at Penzance, he had this portrait taken in John Beringer's Helston studio complete with his new truncheon; note the tall hat, decorated truncheon, and handcuffs carefully arranged on the pedestal. It seems the life of a constable was not for PC Vosper as he resigned not long after, on 13 December 1864.[33]

Above: This mounted albumen photo by Sandry of Camborne shows Sir George Otto Trevelyan laying the corner stone of the Camborne Public Rooms in 1890, during very inclement weather. Every large town seems to have had a public room in Victorian times, something that seems to have gone out of fashion these days. Sir George was a British statesman and author during his ministerial career and Camborne dignitaries must have felt themselves very lucky to have such a personage attending. Sir George was very gracious and said he was very impressed with the state of the Cornish workers' houses during his visit, which he felt necessitated the erection of a public building that should be available for their comfort. Everything that constitutes the legitimate amusements of its workers was a worthy place in their midst, according to the newspaper.

Above: A pair of long demolished thatched cottages at Puggis Hill, Rosewarne, near Camborne; photographed near the end of the nineteenth century, it looks like the lady is in negotiations with a fish jouster. Note how rough the roads were in these days before the motor car and tar macadam were commonplace.

Opposite below: Tin streaming works on the Red River at Rosewarne near Camborne; it is thought this was taken close to the settlement of Roscroggan and looking roughly south towards the area of the Seaton Mines, which are just north of the village of Tuckingmill. At the time this photo was taken, the works look pretty derelict. The stream carried the materials discarded from the mines farther up river; the water from the river was run into long pits and allowed to settle (you can see the pits behind the pool in the foreground). The coarse tin would have been recovered in the mines so the fine grains of ore would be caught by the tin streamer by settlement in these pits. If the river was carrying coarse ore, this would be settled in the preliminary long pits and any sand discarded before overflowing into the main settling pits seen in the foreground. Once settled, it was re-pulped and fed onto the rag frames seen on the right of the image; these would remove some of the tin, which was then moved down to the tin floors for final concentration on round frames and buddles. The Red River flowed on down the valley to exit the land at Godrevy. This is one of the photos that came with the image of Harvey's No. 3 Shed.

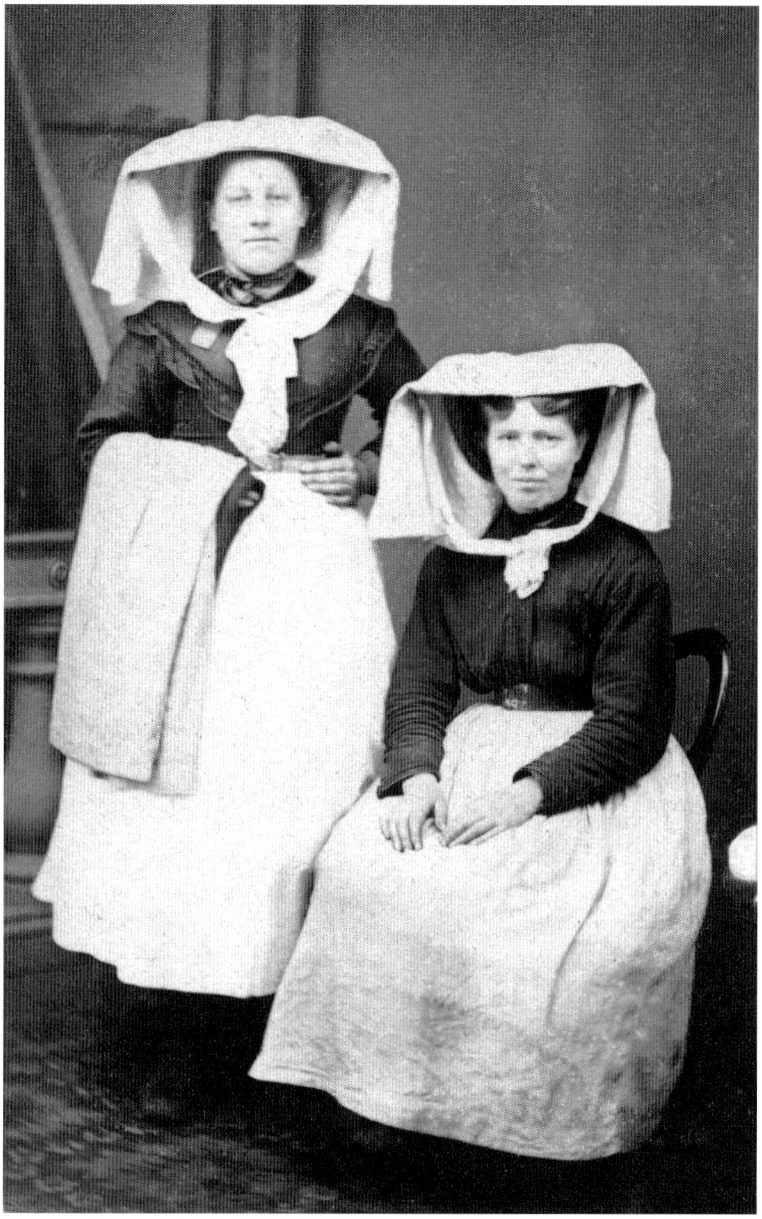

A CdV by John Charles Burrow of Camborne probably taken in the late 1880s of two curiously dressed ladies. These ladies worked at Dolcoath mine in Camborne and are bal maidens. Their distinctive headgear is called a gook; this particular style of gook was referred to as a yard of cardboard so called because of a narrow strip of cardboard inserted under the brim to give it the distinctive shape. Over the arm of the lady on the left is a spare towser; we would know them as aprons that were worn around the waist and wrapped almost all the way around the body. From the 1850s, we read that the whiteness of these towsers were worn as a badge of office and as an indication of your person. Due to the hard, dusty work undertaken, it is quite possible that they wore a clean towser to work and changed into a dirty one before work. The lady on the left is carrying a small bag on her left wrist; they would carry three things into the mine in a small bag: their pasty, crochet or knitting, and a pinch of tea. Apparently, the ladies who worked at Dolcoath had the luxury of the contents of their bags being warmed by a dinner lady in the kitchen shed. The bal maidens worked above grass processing the ore.

A CdV of Carn Brea Castle by James Moody photographer of Fore Street, Redruth. Moody worked mainly in the 1850s and 1860s as a portraitist and very rarely took his camera outdoors, making this image a rarity. The castle was built in 1379 as a chapel dedicated to St Michael; since then, it has been extensively rebuilt by the Basset family and was used as their hunting lodge. The castle is situated 1 mile south-west of Redruth and sits on top of a rocky hill called Carn Brea, a prominent landmark for miles around.

A full-plate photograph of the interior of Camborne parish church, this image was taken before the Victorian restoration took place. The photograph was probably taken by William Piper whose studio was opposite the church; the image was probably taken in the 1850s but definitely before 1862. The church was restored under the supervision of J. Piers St Aubyn, a Cornish architect and restorer; he was commissioned to restore the church in 1859, with work starting in 1862. There is a very similar though not identical image in *Views and Likenesses* probably taken on the same day but from a slightly different angle.[34]

A very early photograph of the humble cottages that once lined Fore Street, Camborne; they were demolished to be replaced by shops. Apparently, the Berrimans shop was built on the site of this cottage. Presumably, this photo was taken by William Piper.

Above: This photo from the late 1870s or early 1880s is of the *Lelant Ferry*, which regularly plied between Lelant near St Ives across the Hayle River. We see the ferryman who I believe to be Tom Gale; he was ferryman for many decades at the oars of his praam, the type of boat that was used to transport his passengers across the river. The praams were built by the ferryman himself and the design copied from the deck boats, which were carried on the Norwegian sailing ships that plied the area. In the background and up river can be seen Lelant Quay; apparently, this area of the river was known as Norway Man's Dock due to the nineteenth-century Norwegian sailing ships that carried timber to be unloaded here and the timber was then floated up river to Harvey's of Hayle.

Below: Hayle Baptists chapel situated in Commercial Road, this photo was taken not long after the chapel was first built, the corner stone being laid on New Year's Day in 1874. The chapel was opened with a special service taken by the Reverend R. Lewis who travelled down from Plymouth for the occasion; he was supported by Wesleyan Minister W. Parkes. On the Monday, there was a public meeting in the chapel with various speakers, which apparently was attended to excess. The chapel continued to be used by the Baptists until it was adapted for Catholic use in 1958.

Above: A CdV by Truro photographer Nicholas Blake Lobb looking back towards St Ives and titled 'View from Tegunna'; a similar and contemporary image is in *Views and Likenesses*.[35] This is taken before the coming of the railway from St Erth in 1873, but better dating evidence is the engine house for West Wheal Providence mine on Pedn Olva Point, the mine being wound up in 1861. The engine house had not been built very long before being converted to a dwelling house. Note all the herring boats on the beach, making for a very interesting and rare image, *c*. 1860.

Below: A cabinet card of St Ives harbour dating from the 1890s. A ketch is moored in centre of the harbour; behind her is another ketch with a backdrop of the St Ives fishing fleet all with their lug sails out drying in this idyllic scene.

Above: A foggy CdV of the St Ives lifeboat RNLB *Covent Garden*, this photograph was taken in the 1870s. She was a ten-oared boat stationed on service at St Ives between 1870 and 1878. St Ives's first lifeboat, *Hope*, came into service in 1840.

Above: The oldest house in St Ives photographed by Valentine in the 1880s and produced as an albumen print. This quaint house is situated in Fish Street just around the corner from the Sloop Inn. Note the ray wings hanging over the front door.

Opposite below: The St Ives flood of 12 November 1894 is dramatically captured on this cabinet card. The torrent is racing down Chapel Street with the Methodist church centre of photo, the force of the white water tumbling down the street and gushing from the sides is captured with great skill. The onlookers understandably look very concerned and serious, which is not surprising as the town had been working for years to make it one of Cornwall's most popular watering holes, as the local paper puts it. The damage to the town was immense with pavements ripped up, as well as services uncovered and destroyed apart from obvious damage to property. An emergency council meeting was held with a resultant disaster fund being started. St Ives was not the only town affected as the paper reports torrents running through many Cornish towns on the same day.

An albumen print of a young boy in his smock sat on the steps outside of Rock House, St Ives, taken by one of Valentine's travelling photographers, *c.* 1880. We can see why the house gets its name, being built into the cliff face that can be seen on the right-hand side of the photo; the cottage is just off of Mount Zion backing onto Fish Street.

The Digey, St Ives captured at the end of the nineteenth century on this atmospheric albumen print. An old fisherman with impressive whiskers, wearing his traditional smock and heavy oilcloth trousers, leans on his porch besides the drying washing while his wife is intently darning when sitting on their steps. Note that the stone near the bottom of the steps has an iron hoop in it; this was a mooring stone used to hold a net, spiller, or long line. As with most of these fishermen's cottages, below the living accommodation was a store for their fishing gear; as it was not part of the living space, the downstairs window has rough wooden shutters.

This is a very interesting pre-1875 albumen print of a much-changed corner of St Ives. On the right, we have the George and Dragon, an inn that was demolished in 1886. Across the street was the Golden Lion; the landlord at this time was Belinda Hosking. The small tiled roof over the door of the Golden Lion is known in Cornwall as a pentice; according to Cyril Noall, it was removed in 1875.

Above: This albumen print dating from the 1870s shows the church and vicarage of St John's in-the-fields and accompanying vicarage; the church is dedicated to St John the Evangelist. The village of Halsetown was the brainchild of the politician and solicitor James Halse, from whom it takes its name. He created and built the parish in the 1830s, although the church shown in this photo was not built until 1857 after the formation of the ecclesiastical parish in 1846.

Below: A beautifully composed late Victorian scene captured on a magic lantern slide; slides like this became popular from the 1890s onwards. The two children on the bridge draw the eye into the photo, which is taken at St Erth. The mill building on the left is Carbis Mill and up the valley can be seen old wooden structures; these are batteries of stamps, which were run by a waterwheel powered by the River Hayle. These stamps were used for crushing the locally mined copper ore; these mines are shown on the 1876 OS map.

Above: This is the Clapper Bridge at St Erth; it was located near Trannack Mill on a metalled road from Carnabeggas to Porthcollumb. The bridge was replaced after the Second World War; adjacent to the bridge there was a ford.

Below: This very early CdV of Zennor was probably taken in the late 1850s, making it probably the oldest known photo of the village; it was taken by St Ives photographer Edward Ashton. Zennor is between St Just and St Ives on the rocky rugged coast. The surrounding countryside is strewn with granite boulders; this local granite was used to build the St Ives and Falmouth granite harbour. A portion of Zennors circular churchyard is visible. On the right, the single-storey building is the blacksmith's shop. The white building to the left of the church is the White House, which was built in 1838. To the left, and at right angles to the White House, is the Tinners Arms. Behind the Tinners Arms, you can see a small roof poking up, this was the horse whim. The large house behind the horse whim is the vicarage.

Above: An early CdV of St John the Baptist's church, Pendeen, it was taken by John Beringer of Helston; the parish was separated from the large parish during the formation of Pendeen Parish, which was originally called North St Just in 1843. Before this present church was built in 1851, the local miners built a wooden church, which was used for three years. When the old wooden church was demolished, the wood was used to floor the present church. This foggy image was probably taken within ten years of the present church being built. Pendeen was a heavily mined area and behind the church can be seen the mine workings of Boscaswell Downs; in fact, the first wooden church was built on the instruction of the vicar Robert Aitken who approached a number of miners on the Platt and said, 'Come on get your picks and shovels we are going to build a church'. They apparently duly complied.

Below: A fantastic CdV taken by John Beringer of Helston in the early 1860s, it shows the dressing floor at Botallack Mine. In the distance can be seen the Crowns and various mine buildings built onto the cliff face. A miner can be seen supervising the dressing floor. Water is running down a wooden launder to power a small waterwheel. I am unsure what it is powering but various settling ponds can be seen in the foreground. A similar contemporary view is featured in *Views and Likenesses* dated 1862.[36]

A full-plate mounted albumen print of Botallack mine probably taken in the late 1850s: remarkably early. It is interesting to note that the buildings at this time were lime-washed. The Crown's Whim can be seen at the top of the cliff, hoisting ore from a platform and operating the copper crusher. Wheal Button engine house can be seen half way down the cliff; to the left of this was a small timber platform. Further down the cliff can be seen a small head frame over Wheal Button itself. On the Crowns is a pumping engine house that was built in 1835 and to its right is the headframe over Crowan's Engine Shaft; the timber of the tramway is just behind it. Boscowan Whim sometimes referred to as Pearce's Whim can be seen just behind them; this powered the rope that hauled the skips up and down the Boscawen Diagonal Shaft, which drops underground at 35 degrees.

This is an early photo, probably taken in 1862 when Button Shaft was first opened as all the timberwork looks new and in very good condition. The image is of the tramway at Botallack going to the mouth of the Boscawen Diagonal Shaft; there is a skip with miners in and another man leaning against the rails. Ore was tipped down onto a platform where it was probably put into kibbles and hauled by the Crown's Whim to the top of the cliff. On the right is a walkway to Wheal Button shaft; it looks like it is uphill, but this is an optical illusion as the shaft drops down at 35 degrees.

Above: This is a cropped portion of the previous photo; we believe it was taken very shortly after the Boscawen Diagonal Shaft was opened, so probably dates to 1862. You can see miners in a skip who have been pulled out of the mine. The photo shows the rollers and wires used to pull the gig and a wooden structure presumably for shelter next to a platform used for embarkation. There appears to be a man at a desk recording who is in the skip. Rollers and wires can be seen behind the wooden structure, with a man wearing white trousers leaning against the fence.

Below: On 24 July 1864, the Prince and Princes of Wales attended Botallack and, donning full mining garb, the party made a decent into the Boscawen Shaft on the wheeled skip. This is how it was described at the time but in reality, what they wore was not the same as the miners, as can be seen by the quality of Princess Alexandra's dress. The mine was gaily decorated with greenery for the event. This photo taken by an unknown photographer (though it is possible Robert Preston had two cameras set up) is taken within seconds of the one in *Views and Likenesses* but from a very slightly different angle, as in this photo we can see the light mounted on the front of the skip. The people in the photo from the front of the skip are Mr St Aubyn and a Danish princess; behind them is Lady St Aubyn, then an unidentified man and woman believed either the Vivians or the Sutherlands; the Prince of Wales is behind the gentleman and the brakeman is Captain John Rowe. This tramway will be shown in other photos in this book.[37]

Princess Alexandra in her mining attire complete with specimen hammer. Note the fine embroidery on her dress. I have another, taken on the same day, of her seated holding her hammer in the same mining attire. The photograph is taken on the battlements of St Michael's Mount in 1865. The CdV was one of a series produced commercially by Robert Preston of Penzance who was the official photographer for the visit.[38]

A wonderful stereoview sold by Spreat of Exeter dating from 1858 if not slightly earlier, Professor Thomas suggests it may have been taken by one of the Beringer brothers.[39] It depicts the walkway round to Button Shaft complete with its head frame and associated structures. The walkway is the structure above the tramway. There appears to be a lot of work going on with a small tram on the walkway and a chute to take material to a lower level, together with loose planks and a ladder on the walkway. This was probably taken before the tramway or the diagonal shaft was constructed. Some work is going on at the entrance to the diagonal shaft which is covered by shuttering and can be seen below and to the left of the walkway. By 1860, the rails had been laid in the Boscawen Shaft down to the 100-fathom mark, assuming that the tramway could be used to ship materials for construction in and out of the Diagonal Shaft. They had started laying the rails in October 1859, but work began on the shaft in 1858, suggesting this as the most appropriate date for this remarkable image.

Charles Renowden Lobb from Egloshayle, St Breock, was a professional photographer who took this great image; strangely, he seems to have worked mainly in the west of Cornwall many miles from his home in north Cornwall. He was born in 1841 and sadly had a very short life; he was dead by the age of thirty so any of his images were taken before 1871. This CdV is from the early 1860s and is of the tramway into the Boscawen Diagonal shaft; you can clearly see the 35-degree angle of the shaft. Halfway down you can see the skip on its descent; it is possible that this could have been the royal party although there is no evidence of any decoration which was prominent for their visit in 1865. The wooden combing at the lower end of the track is for protection from the sea, which sprayed up from the waves breaking on the cliff below.

Above: An early CdV-sized paper print taken before 1875, it was obviously never mounted on card which is a shame as it may have survived in better condition. It is a rare early view of St Just United Mines. I am not sure if the crowd is for the camera or whether the man standing in the centre was addressing the throng; I have been told it was taken on a payday. Cape Cornwall can be seen in the background, the white building on the right was the count house, and the stack on the right was for Weston's engine. Apparently, the mine was made up of several smaller mining properties: Nanpean, Ballowal, and Bosorne.[40] At the time this photo was taken, around 800 men were employed at the mine.

Below: This full-plate mounted albumen print was taken by Gibson in 1889 of the Cunard cargo vessel *Malta*. She was aground on the cliffs at Lenidjack Castle, Cape Cornwall. In the background can be seen Botallack Mine. The *Malta* was built by J. and G. Thompson of Glasgow, she was launched on 9 October 1865 and entered service on 20 February 1866. On her final voyage, she left Liverpool for Genoa on 14 October 1889 with a full complement of passengers plus 2,000 tons of general cargo. The following day, she foundered on the rocks of the Cornish coast.

Above: This CdV by Trembath of St Just is of Alma Villa (now Penrose House); it was taken in the 1860s not long after the house was built for Stephen James Harvey; he and both his sons have memorials in the local parish church. They had mining interests at Botallack, which was not far from their house. The house at one time had a large grand entrance on to the road, which has long since gone; although the granite garden walls are surmounted by iron railings stamped Holman. Apparently being within sight of the bridge, it was the meeting place for the men and youngsters of the village; they would sit on the stones against the wall and spin yarns and often make music. Apparently, boys would turn a clothes line into a skipping rope, while girls skipped the men would play a tune on the concertina, but those days are long gone; today, there is still a seat under the walls of the house where the traveller can sit and rest their weary legs.

Below: The first and last house at Land's End, this CdV was produced by Robert Preston after the royal visit to Botallack so shortly after 1865. Grace Thomas, the originator of this business, is standing in the doorway alongside tourists who also pose for the photograph. Rock specimens on the table are for sale as souvenirs.[41] On an academic point, I have seen this same image produced as a stereoview by W. Brooks, photographer Penzance numbered 153: I wonder who actually took it?

Above: The Land's End Hotel, an albumen print made in the 1870s or 1880s showing the Royal Mail coach, which says on it St Buryan, Land's End. This would have been the main means of transport for the tourists coming down by train to Penzance to the hotel. It is said that in the 1870s, there could be as many as 100 people per day visiting Land's End. Packed wagons made trips from outside the Queens Hotel, Penzance. Daily excursions were made to Land's End and the Logan Rock. At the time this photo was taken, Thomas Toman was the proprietor of the hotel; he took it over in 1873 after his brother Edwin Toman took over the First and Last Inn in Sennen from Thomas.

Below: Taken in the early 1880s, outside of the Queens Hotel, Penzance waits one of Champion's brakes loaded with passengers ready for a day out to Logan Rock and Land's End. There was a lot of competition between rivalling tours, although there were enough tourists that they were always pretty full.

A wonderful study of the old Longships Lighthouse, which was taken from a ship by Wadebridge photographer C. R. Lobb. It is a full-plate albumen print, but I also have CdVs of a very similar image without the people in; it appears he took at least three photographs probably to make sure he had a successful image, having the movement of the boat to contend with. The photo taken in the late 1850s or very early 1860s is of the first Longships Lighthouse, which was 78 feet high.[42]

Two men in a buggy outside of the entrance to Star Castle overlooking Hugh Town on St Mary's, Isles of Scilly. This photo taken in the 1870s by John Gibson was produced on CdV-sized albumen paper and was never mounted onto card. The Star Castle was built by Robert Adams in 1593; he was surveyor of the royal works, under the supervision of the Captain of the Islands Francis Godolphin. The fort was built on the instruction of Elizabeth I following the Spanish Armada of 1588; she was worried there could be another attack on her realm.

A beautifully composed full-plate albumen print taken in the 1880s of the Holy Vale on St Mary's, Isles of Scilly.

An early CdV of Hugh Town harbour by John Carvosso Tonkin. This photographer is first recorded in 1873 but I believe he took this photo in the late 1860s.[43] The Star Castle can be seen on the hill on the left. It certainly had a commanding view over the harbour and sound; there is a similar view by Gibson in *Views and Likenesses*.[44]

An albumen print of Hugh Town, St Mary's, from below the Star Castle looking across the town. On the left is Town Beach and on the right is Porthcressa Beach. In the distance with the windmill on the summit is Buzza Hill; the windmill has no sails, dating it to after 1880. The tall building in the centre is the parish church (consecrated in 1838). Two large vessels are being built on stocks on Town Beach; the yard was booming when John Gibson took this photo in the early 1880s.

An albumen print probably by F. E. Gibson, as it is very similar to and from the same spot as an earlier image featured in *Views and Likenesses*.[45] In July 1870, France declared war on Prussia and the German States. As luck would have it, a fleet of German merchant men were anchored in the Sound. This photo is titled in contemporary hand 'Town of St Mary's with war bound German ships in the Roads Sept 1870'. On this occasion, I have left the original annotation on the photo, which describes the scene perfectly. Along the top are the names of each of the islands in the background.

Above: Tresco Abbey photographed by John Gibson in the mid-1870s from the south; shrubs and plants on the rock garden are by this time quite established.[46] Tresco's original twelfth-century abbey stood in the gardens of the present house and the garden has been cleverly designed around their ruins. The house was built by Augustus Smith; he started building in 1835 with further additions being made in 1843, 1861, and 1891. The house was built using roughly coursed granite and a slate roof, some of the timbers and panelling in the house came from local shipwrecks.

Below: St Levan's church from the south. The driver of the covered wagon looks suspiciously at the unfamiliar camera. This is an ancient Christian site with a wattle and thatched building being erected by St Leven in the fourth century on the site of the present alter. This was superseded in the twelfth century by the traditional cruciform-shaped building, which stood on the site of the present nave back to the tower. In the fifteenth century, the church was extended to its present-day form, yet the tower is believed to be older than the fifteenth century. A holy well is also associated with the chapel along with the ancient St Leven stone and six Celtic crosses.

Above: An albumen print of Porthgwarra Cove taken by one of Valentine's travelling photographers in the 1880s. This cove is privately owned and lies within the parish of St Leven. A couple of Porthgwarra crabbers are moored on chains that ran up the beach. The vessel in the foreground with three fishermen working on their gear is the *Good Templar* PZ 256. She was 19 feet long with two masts. The forward mast would be lowered when beached. She was lugger-rigged and owned by James and Robert Jackson of Porthgwarra between 1884 and 1891 when she was sold to the Fowey district.

Below: This stereoview half from the late 1870s shows an image of a Cornish roundhouse. This building has long since been demolished; it was on the road to Land's End at Crows-an-Wra. At one time, it was a little shop catering to the tourists; at the time this photo was taken, there is no evidence of tourism judging by the pair of pigs eating at the trough outside of the front door.

Nancothan Watermill as it was in 1867. This beautiful unattributed albumen print shows the semi derelict overshot mill; it was situated just upstream of Buryas Bridge, south-west of Penzance.[47]

Above: The parish church of St Buryan, being mainly constructed in the fifteenth century, is located within the centre of the village of the same name. In front of the church can be seen one of St Buryan's six crosses. A church has stood on the site since at least 930, when Saint Buriana's chapel was patronised by King Athelstan. The Royal Mail coach that we saw earlier in the book outside of the Land's End Hotel is obviously on another of its scheduled stops; curiously what looks to be the same barrel is on the roof: was it the same day or was the barrel used for some permanent purpose?

Below: A very early CdV that dates from the early 1860s, it depicts the First and Last Inn at Sennen. Proudly advertised on its wall was that the landlord was Thomas Toman. He was later to move to the Land's End Hotel in 1873 to be replaced here as landlord by his brother, Edwin.

Above: In this photograph by Gibson of Penzance, you can see a cart outside of St Buryan's churchyard; this was used to transport bodies from the wreck of the Atlantic Transport Company's SS *Mohegan*. She was wrecked on 14 October 1898. After leaving London for New York with 57 passengers and 103 crew, she ran ashore off the Lizard between the Manacles and the Lowlands; the ship struck Vase Rock and drifted onto Maen Varses reef. The passengers were having dinner and were unaware of the accident and the severity of their plight. The seas were rough and many of the passengers and crew were washed off of the taffrail. Of the 200 persons on board, only thirty-one survived. The dead were buried in a mass grave in St Buryan churchyard.

Below: Drift Village, 2 miles west of Penzance in the parish of Sancreed. This photo was taken by Victorian artist A. R. Q. Quinton in 1894 during a research and inspirational trip for his series of paintings from Land's End to John O'Groats.

Above: Penzance photographer Robert Preston took this idyllic view around 1880; looking down over the fishing village of Mousehole framed by its ancient harbour walls. The port's most notable event was being destroyed by the Spanish raid of 1595.

Below left: A lovely albumen photo of the Keigwin Arms, as it was called when this photo was taken in 1879. Despite the appearance of being a random gathering of locals, the scene has been carefully staged with a fish wife's cowal and a random cannon ball on the cobbles, an obvious reference to the attack by the Spanish raid fwhen Squire Jenkyn Keigwin was killed on 23 July 1595 while defending his house.

Below right: Taken in the 1880s, this albumen print shows the road out of Newlyn towards Mousehole. To the left on Penlee Point can be seen the abandoned chimney stack of Wheal Tolvadden Mine.

A wonderful pair of photos by Penzance photographer John Gibson, probably taken in the late 1870s; they show the old medieval harbour of Newlyn prior to the start of building the present-day Newlyn harbour. South Pier, the one with the lighthouse on, was started in 1885 and completed in 1886. After its completion, the North Pier was started, with its first half being completed by 1888; the whole pier was finished by 1894. In the background is Gwavas Lake with the mackerel fleet at anchor. In the foreground, the bustling scene is caused by the activity around the fish that have been caught; after being landed by punts onto the beach, ready to be auctioned. Fishwives, with their cowals and distinctive shawls, alongside fish jousters, are driving their Callington carts, which line the beach within old Newlyn harbour.

Above: This early photo of Penzance was taken from the Alexandra Terrace looking across the Lariggan and Folly Fields; it is taken before the building of Bodilly's Flour Mill in 1874. Working from right to left, the building with the colonnade to its left-hand side was the Norton's Royal Baths; to the left of the baths is the western end of the Queen's Hotel; to the left and on the skyline is the distinctive St Mary's church. In the left foreground can be seen the Alexandra Dairy and above the dairy can be seen the new houses in Redinnick; on the skyline above them is the Methodist chapel.

Below: This image scanned from a magic lantern slide was photographed within the medieval harbour of Newlyn during the late 1890s. A beautiful scene of day-to-day life in a Victorian fishing harbour, a crew from a fishing boat have just sculled ashore after mooring up their vessel. They are dressed in their traditional white smocks. Above them can be seen the Anglican church's Fishermen's Rest, a meeting and reading room for the fishermen when not at sea. In the foreground are several mackerel boats, including PZ 43 *Myra*; she is a real old timer, being originally registered before the present-day PZ registration, originally registered under the pre-1869 PE registration. Her owners at this time were John Tremethick and Thomas Rodda; she was skippered by Thomas Tremethick. Built as an open 40-foot-long boat before being fully decked when she was sold to Philip Cotton in 1886, her registration was cancelled in 1900.

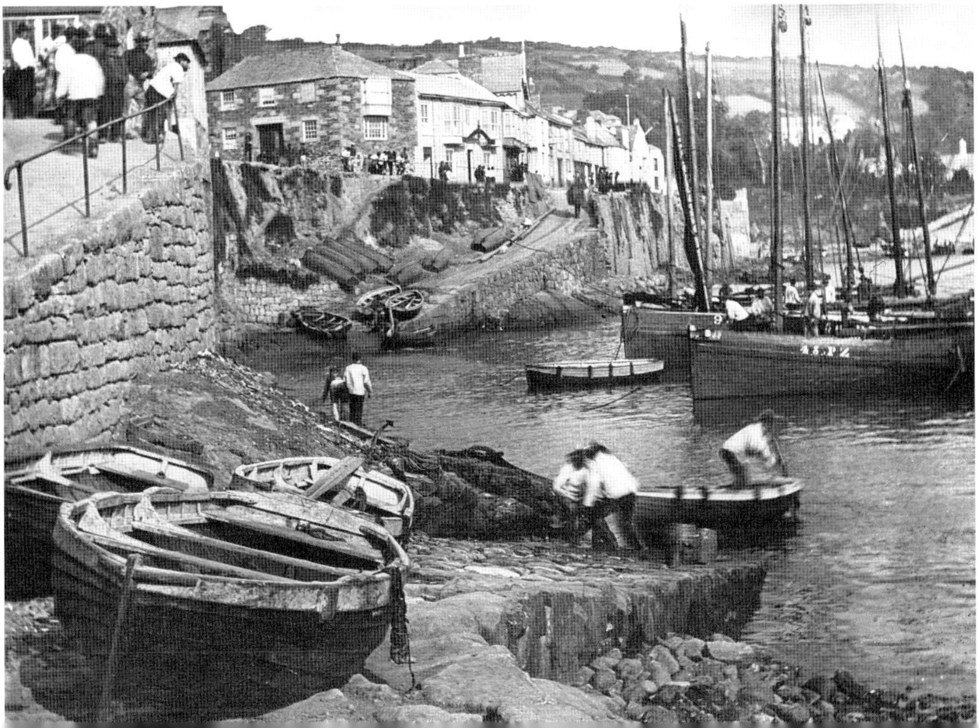

Above: Penzance Promenade can be seen in the distance; in the foreground is Newlyn harbour, which is dominated by Newlyn North Pier. Between the masts of the sailing ship can be seen the church tower of St Mary the Virgin, Penzance. The sailing ship is a three-masted wooden barque; she is riding high in the water so will have discharged her cargo. To the left alongside the pier are two Lowestoft drifters; above them on the quay wall are piles of wooden fish boxes. In the foreground is a gaff-rigged pilchard boat. The mackerel fleet is at sea, evident by their punt lying on the moorings in the safety of the harbour. Newlyn North Pier was built in stages: The first half is a full-width pier and was completed in 1886; the second half was a breakwater and is seen on the right of the image before it was widened in 1907. The absence of steam drifters suggests a date of before 1900.

Below: A glass magic lantern slide taken in the 1890s of the top of the North Pier Newlyn where the mackerel market, which was built around 1901 or 1902 is now located. Left of foreground is a slope that leads down to the harbour. The catch was transported up from the bummers' gigs. These were punts that were used to row the fish ashore from the moored fishing vessels. In the background can be seen various fish sellers' offices; apparently, Hobson's hut was thrown into the harbour during the fish riots of May 1896.

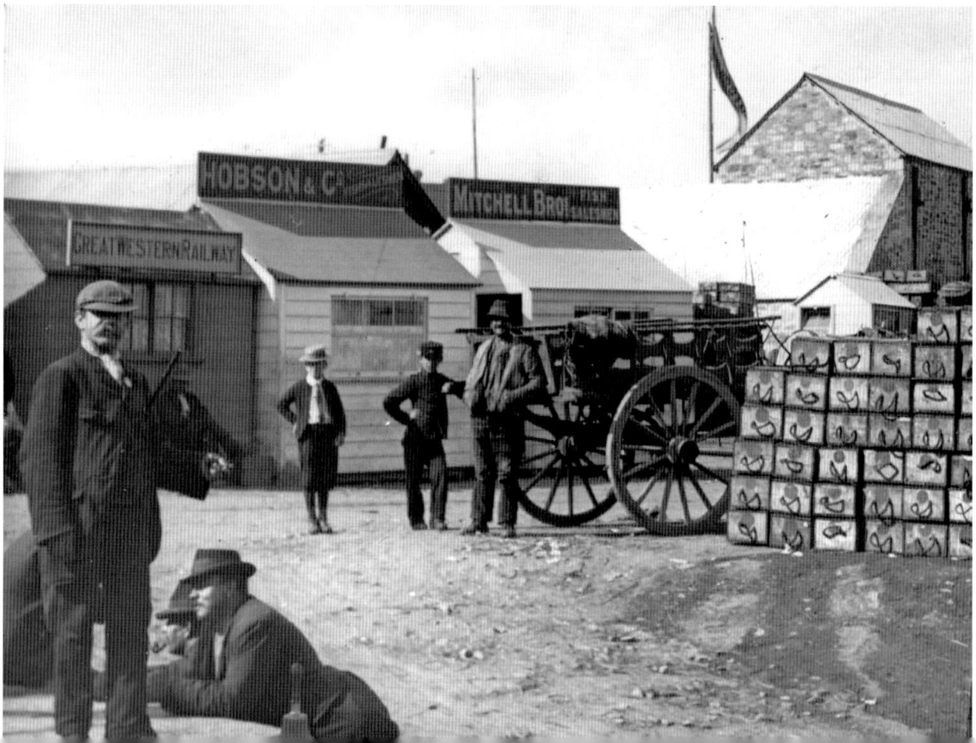

Above: Photographed in the late 1890s, this glass magic lantern slide shows Newlyn old harbour; the slope on the left leads up from the old harbour to the higher part of Newlyn. On the right is the Strand, which leads onto Street-an-Nowan—the lower part of the village. The small boats moored in front of the Strand are pilchard boats; the large industrial building on the left of the Strand was used for classes such as the making of Newlyn Copper. Next to the smaller pilchard boats are two larger mackerel boats. PZ 448 was the *Jane Reid*, built at Newlyn in 1878 for Michael Thomas; she was 48 feet long and skippered by Christopher Thomas. The capstan on the *Jane Reid* is just aft of her number; these capstans were used for hauling the foot lines of their nets, enabling the boats to in effect pull themselves along their nets as they were hauling.

Below: A scan of a glass magic lantern slide taken around 1894 just after the harbour was completed. In this image we are looking towards the Narrows with the slope down to the South Pier on the left. The boats moored in the right foreground are mackerel boats; there are other mackerel boats to the left. The fact that the boats are covered suggests the season has finished and the boats are laid up and not fishing. The boat nearest the camera is PZ 147 *Favorite*; she was 46.2 feet long weighing in at 23 tons and was built at Newlyn in 1875 for a local, Sally Kelynack. She was skippered by John Williams and broken up in 1910.

Above: The higher part of Newlyn Town in the 1890s taken from a glass magic lantern slide. The slope on the left leads down past a sail maker's workshop on towards the old harbour where mackerel boats are moored; nets are drying over the handrail while on the other side of the slope are a string of cork floats, which are attached to the head of the net. The road to the right goes through the Narrows and again emerges on the cliff, which was a favoured spot for the fishermen to lean on the railings and have a yarn.

Below: Trewarveneth Street Newlyn looking down towards the slip and harbour. This idyllic scene was taken in the 1890s by the brilliant Victorian professional photographer Owen Graystone Bird, he worked out of Bath; he would have carefully composed the scene with the mawns and Cornish knit-frock on the left and the children talking to the lady on the right.

Above: A full-plate albumen print of St Peter's church, the Coombe, and Newlyn, taken in the 1880s. In the background behind the boy leaning on the railings can be seen the vicarage. The octagonal bell tower in the foreground was topped out in 1906 and the North aisle was added in1886; neither of these additions had taken place when this photo was taken.

Below: An albumen print taken in the 1870s showing Street-an-Nowan and Newlyn town from Devil's Rock, Tolcarne. The large building in the right foreground is St Peter's church, which was built between 1864 and 1866; this church is seen from the other side in the previous photo. Beside and to the left of the church can be seen the back of Tolcarne farm house. On the right beyond the church lies the imposing Vivian House. Behind its pair of chimneys are the glass houses of Chypons Villa, which housed the vinery. The front of the villa itself is up the hill to the right. In the centre of the photo can be seen Clifton Terrace, with the hotchpotch of houses and roofs of Street-an-Nowan and Fradgan; these lead to the medieval pier and Newlyn Town. In the distance can be seen Penlee Point and the chimney stack of the abandoned Wheal Tolvadden mine; also, on the hillside is Gwavas Quarry in its early days.

Above: Robert Preston of Penzance took this photograph looking back on Newlyn harbour, taken from Tolcarne shortly after it was completed in 1894. On the right can be seen Chypons Villa and Trinity Chapel. In the distance on the hillside can be seen the beginnings of Gwavas Quarry, with Wheal Tolvadden Mine chimney stack on Penlee Point.

Opposite: This glass slide was taken in the 1890s by Richard Preston of Penzance; it shows two local Penzance characters: Billy Renfree and his wife, Janie. The photo is taken under Champion's Slip in the corner of Newlyn harbour. Here Billy would have bought fish direct from the local boats and travelled around the locality selling from door to door; he was what is known locally as a fish jouster. He was a well-photographed character of his day with his bushy beard and distinctive ringlets, which at the time of this photo were still black. In the background can be seen work being undertaken on a lugger, which is difficult to identify with certainty but is believed to be the *Alarm* PZ 24.

Penzance and Newlyn were famous for their fishwives. These ladies were numerous and carried distinctive wicker or withy baskets on their backs, which were supported by a strap that went across the forehead, these cowals (cowls or baskets) were used to carry fish. The most famous of the fishwives was Mary Kelynack, a local character who walked to London and back for the great Exhibition of 1851 where she presented a pound of tea to Queen Victoria and Prince Albert. She duly noted this in her diary; this journey took her five weeks. This photograph is a studio portrait taken by Penzance photographer Robert Preston of Lizzie Glasson (*née* Tonkin) with her cowal, adorned in her traditional workaday clothes.

This is a famous full-plate albumen print by John Gibson taken in the 1880s. The photo shows Elizabeth Lanyon standing and Blanch Courtney sitting giving Betsy a pinch of snuff. The photo is obviously staged in Gibson's Penzance studio; photographers seemed to love the old fishwives for their portraits, and presumably they were more popular images for the booming tourist trade.

Four portraits of Newlyn fishwives: Top left is Blanch Courtney with her cowal, you can clearly see the strap that went across her forehead; the other three are unidentified—if anyone knows who they are, please let me know. The top left is an albumen print, top right a cabinet card, and the other two were produced as CdVs; all were commercially available to the wealthy tourists of the 1860s and '70s.

A very early CdV of the Promenade, the Promenade runs along the seafront at Penzance. This image was taken by Wadebridge photographer Charles Renowden Lobb and photo can be dated reasonably accurately to between 1865 and 1868. There is no turret on the Queen's Hotel so that dates it to before the new building was constructed in 1871, coincidentally the year the photographer died. The lifeboat house, which was built in 1863, is evident, dating it to being after 1863. Many thanks to the local historians who identified these two points that help date the image.

A dramatic CdV by Robert Preston of Penzance; he was obviously out and about with his camera on this stormy day before 1877. This photograph was taken before Preston's competitor, the marvellous photographer John Gibson started working from the building; we know this as there is no Gibson sign in the window, suggesting that it is before Gibson's occupation. The photo shows a wave breaking on the promenade in front of the Royal Baths; the Royal Baths have wooden shutters pulled over the windows and the basement gratings as protection from the elements.

Above: The Esplanade, or Promenade at Penzance in the early 1890s. Everyone is out for a stroll on the prom in their Sunday best. The railings seen in the photo were replaced in 1897 for the Queen Victoria's Jubilee, so the photograph is definitely taken before 1897.

Below: This interesting full-plate albumen print was taken around 1880 or 1881. The old sea wall, most of which was swept away in 1880, is being repaired in the background. This image was taken from Mount View Terrace, Jacks Lane (now called Chywoon Lane). In the foreground, the dominant building is the Trinity Methodist Chapel, which was built in 1834. Just to the right is the Old Bridge House, this house was destroyed by fire in 1894: note the pilot's tower on the roof; the building fronted the housing in Florence Place. The right foreground shows part of the orchard where the Kenstella Estate was later built. In the mid-distance, you can see the western end of Alexandra Terrace; Bodilly's Flour Mill, Lariggan, which was built in 1874; and the serpentine works at Wherrytown; the Esplanade can be seen running below Bodilly away to the right.

Above: Outside Dingley's Private Hotel and Boarding House situated on the Promenade at Penzance. These very large Jersey cars were pulled by a team of four horses on day trips to Logan Rock and Land's End. This car is proudly signed 'Warrens Excursions Car'; remarkably, it seems to be holding about thirty people. Brakes as opposed to Jersey cars were also used for the same excursions, starting at the Queens Hotel.

Below: The Abbey, a seven-bedroom house, dates from 1660 and overlooks the harbour of Penzance, the building was photographed and produced as a CdV in 1878. The house is still recognisable to this day, although the wrought iron railings have been replaced by a high stone wall and the walls are now painted blue; the house is now open to parties and guests.

Above: This fantastic full-plate albumen print was taken by John Gibson in the 1860s looking up Quay Street. The midsummer fair was traditionally held on this precarious pitch overhanging Penzance harbour walls; a few onlookers can be seen outside their regular haunts looking at the fairs various stalls and rides. The distinctive building on the corner was the harbour office, which was removed to allow a road through connecting the quay to the Promenade. This photograph can be dated to within a few years as the blocks of Lamorna granite on the right are bound for the building of the Wolf Rocks Lighthouse and were worked on the old quay and shipped out between 1861 and 1869, giving good dating evidence to this image.[48]

Opposite above: This is a late nineteenth-century photo of Penzance floating dock, which was completed in 1894. This atmospheric photograph was taken by local photographer Robert Preston. On the right is a three-masted barque with a small ketch astern of her. On either side of the dock gates are the capstans, which were used to open the gates. On the right is the road across the harbour with the Ross Bridge giving access to the dry dock; the bridge was named after local banker and MP C. C. Ross.

Opposite below: Penzance harbour from Lescudjack taken in the 1890s by William Harrison of Falmouth. In the background is the floating harbour, which opened in 1884. To the right of the harbour, the dark circular structure is the gasworks and gas holder; centre left of the photo can be seen the Albert Pier pointing out into the bay. Beyond the man leaning on the gate can be seen the distinctive roof of Penzance railway station; far left can be seen the Lighthouse Pier with a two-funnelled paddle steamer lying alongside it.

Above: This very early full-plate albumen print is of an earlier engraving, it is pasted on the same album page as the image below, showing the same location thirty years later; note that this is prior to the building of the Three Tuns Hotel. This image shows the Green Market and the corner of Causewayhead with the Market Cross in its original position on the corner of the street. The image is annotated in contemporary hand on the album page: 'Market Cross in its original position, removed in 1825 to the position shown below'.

Below: A wonderful early image of the Green Market and corner of Causewayhead, Penzance, it was taken by local photographer Robert Preston; according to Professor Charles Thomas, this is Preston's earliest dated photograph, taken in 1860.[49] This full-plate albumen print is glued onto a Victorian album page; it has written beneath it in contemporary hand: 'The Green Market Penzance showing the Market Cross. Hemmings Three Tuns Hotel discontinued 1867, and Mr Richards Pawnshop, as I remember them about 1850'.

This CdV of St Mary the Virgin, Penzance, was taken about thirty years after it was built in 1835. The previous church was demolished due to it being too small to house the congregation; the Reverend Thomas Vyvyan was responsible for the demolition of the old church and building of a new one. The interior of the present-day church was badly damaged by fire in 1986. The organ casing is worth noting as it is dated 1676 and came from St Mary's in Oxford.

Above: This unattributed photograph of Market Jew Street, Penzance was taken during the 1870s or 80s. It must be winter as all the horses have coats or blankets on. Symons'chemist shop is prominent on the left and the photograph was taken after the Humphrey Davey statue was erected in 1872; the statue was made by Wills of London out of white marble.

Below: This full-plate albumen print was taken before the Penzance floating dock was built in 1884; it shows the battery of cannon that were overlooking Penzance station and goods yard. Behind the battery were a row of coastguard cottages and it has been suggested that the occupants of these manned the guns. These cottages were later demolished and replaced by a row of terraced houses. The railway came to Penzance in 1852 and in this photo, the goods sheds can be seen in the centre with the passenger station centre right.

Above: This foggy early photograph is one half of a stereoview; it shows some old cottages, and above them the Old Inn that stood in Gulval. It was demolished in the late 1800s, being replaced with the present-day public house, the Coldstreamer, along with a small estate of houses around it. Gulval is a parish 1 mile from Penzance.

Below: Half of an early stereoview showing the eighteenth-century inn King William IV in Madron as approached from Heamoor, this image was probably taken in the 1880s. The buildings in the background have changed out of all recognition, but the pub is still recognisable.

Above: A stereoview by William Brooks of Penzance, it was taken either in the late 1850s or early 1860s. Although it is a very foggy image, I have included it as it is a very rare early image of what was at the time the vicarage in Gulval. The house is still standing but the veranda has now sadly gone, the house now being a very smart private residence. In 1856, the vicarage is listed as worth £365 rent charge per year with residence and 20 acres of glebe land, in the gift of the Lord Chancellor; the Rev. W. W. Wingfield, BA, is the incumbent.[50]

Below: St Michael's Mount situated within Mount's Bay is one of the most photographed buildings in the county and has been so since photography was invented. This is a particularly early CdV where the unknown photographer has tried to use some very well-dressed people and a fishwife to frame St Michael's Mount by sitting them on the rocks and punts in the foreground.

Above: A full-plate mounted albumen photograph dated on its mount in ink as from 1869, but it could be much earlier as the shrubbery and paths are almost identical with William Jenkyn's photograph of 1857.[51] This image is taken from the north-west side of the Mount looking up at the church. Images can often be earlier than the dates written on them, the reason being the prints were produced commercially and sometimes held in stock for a long while; the tourist would buy the photograph to paste in their album page, which they would annotate and date.

Below: An early 1860s CdV by Charles Renowden Lobb of Wadebridge, he photographed the Mount extensively. This view is taken before the Victorian alteration to this side of the Mount, which took place during the 1870s.

Charles Renowden Lobb of Wadebridge seems to have been a prolific photographer of St Michael's Mount; one can only assume they were all taken on the same visit as it is a very long way from his home town of Wadebridge on the north coast. Here he is taking a photo looking up at the Castle from the harbour wall, capturing half of the *Lord Riverston* in the process.[52] I expect he cursed the boat for being in the way at the time, but it now provides an atmospheric frame to the portrait.

Above: A fantastic very early image of St Michaels Mount, it stands imposingly above the village and harbour. A ketch is dried out on the firm bed of the harbour with a horse cart in attendance presumably unloading goods. It is surprising how large the ships were that plied this little community.

Below: An albumen print taken in the 1880s by Valentine, of Prussia Cove, which is on the eastern side of Mount's Bay on the Lizard. Prussia Cove was made famous by the wrecker and smuggler John Carter who was born in 1738. He and his two brothers, Harry and Charles, were prolific smugglers. John, a staunch Wesleyan, was known as the King of Prussia and wrote an autobiography called *The Autobiography of a Cornish Smuggler.* John had a remarkable resemblance to Frederick the Great; who was King of Prussia, hence John's nickname, with his notoriety gradually transferring to the cove's name. The cottage with the three roof windows is Cliff Cottage, which was the Carters' headquarters in the eighteenth century. The big house in the centre is Sea View House and the thatched cottage to the left is Willy's Cottage, which was named after an old fisherman who lived in it called Willy Brake.

This is a late Victorian studio portrait of two young miners from Breage, a village on the Lizard 3 miles from Helston. I find this photo quite comical as the two miners, who are obviously very young and dressed in their very clean miners' clothes, complete with hard felt hat and carrying tallow candles has been doctored either with make up or more likely by the photographer painting on the negative, giving them moustaches; it does however perfectly illustrate how the miners of the day would have been dressed to go to do a hard day's graft.

Above: A very large format-mounted albumen print taken on 8 May during the 1880s of Grylls Monument, Helston, on Flora Day, otherwise known as the Feast of St Michael's. Under the monument are the dancers who took part in the Helston Furry Dance and their accompanying band, which was probably the Helston Town band. The dance is to commemorate the passing of winter and coming of spring. The dancers traditionally wear Lily of the Valley, with the gents on the left facing up and the ladies on the right facing down; at the time this photo was taken, these traditions were not so rigidly followed.

Below left and right: The photograph on the left is a stereoview of Penhellis taken in the 1860s. I know that this photo shows very little, but it is a very rare image and needs recording as does the photo on the right of Penrose Lodge, Helston. Penhellis in Cross Street, Helston is not mentioned in the 1856 *Kelly's Directory* but by 1873, it was the residence of Frederick Hill Esquire, though I think this image probably dates from the late 1860s. Penrose Lodge, also scanned from a stereoview dating from the 1860s, is situated on Penrose Hill and is listed as Helston Lodge with mention of some aspects of the house being seventeenth century and presumed to have originally come from the local manor house.

Above: This albumen print of Gunwalloe church probably dates from the early 1870s; the church is situated in Gunwalloe church cove and is noted for its detached bell tower, which is not obvious from this photo. This photo was taken before the tamarisk grew up around the churchyard, so the south-east-facing cove can clearly be seen in the background. In this photo, the entrance to the churchyard has a stout wall with granite capping where a coffin could be rested, followed by low steps into the churchyard; this has all now been demolished.

Below: Looking from the south-west towards Helston, this late Victorian unattributed albumen print shows St Michael's church top left; just below the church is a row of cottages that have been demolished since this photo was taken. The building with the arches underneath it is the Masonic Hall. In the bottom left can be seen the gasworks; the round gas holder is now the site of the Church of Jesus Christ of the Latter-day Saints, opposite Lidl.

Above: Porthcurnow Eastern Cable Office Station before it was extended; this is a very early view of this famous building captured on a CdV. This is the terminus for the submarine cables that were laid by Brunel's *Great Eastern*; the cables were to relay telegraph signals from other countries around the Empire. In 1872, the Eastern Telegraph Company was formed; this took over the operation of the cables and built the cable office in the valley at Porthcurnow.

Below: This CdV shows Porthcurnow Eastern Cable Office Station captured in the 1890s after it had been extended and recreational facilities added. Here we can see the tennis courts and another wing to the building; I also know they had a football team so there must have been quite a few people working here to support such activities.

Above: An albumen print taken inside the Porthcurnow Eastern C. O. Station in the 1890s—a very rare insight into the workings of this building that revolutionised communication around the world from the Lizard Cornwall. These buildings are now the Porthcurnow Telegraph Museum.

Below: A picnic on the Lizard captured by the photographer H. T. Ashby. He was an amateur photographer who in 1886 put together an album of large format photographs of mainly the Roseland Peninsula presumably while staying in the area. This is a skilful composition of the tourists who have had a nice picnic on the Lizard and are making their precarious way back down to the waiting punt, picnic baskets in hand, to be rowed back to the steam launch.

Above: The following three very early CdVs, all taken by J. Beringer, are of Kynance Cove, but they are not all of the same date. I am not sure which is the oldest, but they could be as early as the late 1850s. This particular CdV is looking back towards the Cove from the valley. Note the wooden bridge across the river; in this image, there is a little ladder down to the river and crude wooden handrails on the bridge. On top of Henry Essex's refreshment house, situated on the left with the double gables, there is a peculiar structure on the roof at its western end. I am not sure what it is, but it is not in the other photos.

Below: In this CdV of Henry Essex's refreshment house, the western end of the building has no strange feature as in the last photo. Tables are out for customers to use and a well-worn path winds its way up the rugged cliffs. This image is a cropped portion of a portrait-shaped CdV of the road to Kynance, probably one of the earliest known images of Kynance.

Above: Another very early CdV of Kynance Cove, probably dating from the 1850s, showing the western end of the refreshment house run by Henry Essex, later to become Olver's refreshment house. They heavily extended it. Again, there is no sign of the strange structure on the roof in the previous photo. The wooden bridge has no ladder and no handrails, and in the background are Lizard Point and Lion Rock.

Below: A CdV taken in the 1860s by Wadebridge photographer C. R. Lobb of the Lizard Lighthouse on Lizard Point, it is the most southerly point on the British mainland, so it is unsurprising that a light was erected here as early as 1619 by Sir John Killigrew. It was demolished in 1630 due to difficulties funding and maintaining it. The present lighthouses were built as a pair of towers separated by a row of cottages as can be seen in the image. When this photo was taken, both towers were lit but since 1903, only the eastern tower has remained in use; the lighthouse is still in use to this day, but there has been no lighthouse keeper since automation in 1998.

A mounted albumen photograph taken by the Falmouth photographer William Tregaskis. This atmospheric image shows the renovations of St Keverne's church being undertaken in 1893. The Victorians were compulsive renovators of our parish churches; here the workmen have momentarily stopped work to pose for the photographer.

Above: Cadgwith Cove, showing the beach in the late 1880s. We can see the small crabbing boats in the foreground while in the background are two seine boats with their nets ready to shoot, being protected under a tarpaulin. These could be used for catching any of the shoal fish such as mackerel, herring, or pilchards; mackerel and herring would have been salted down or stored in brine and used as bait for crabbing. The fishermen would have used the seine boats like a cooperative as they all needed to work together to man these large boats as bait needed to be caught in the summer and stored to be used throughout the rest of the year.

Opposite above: Cadgwith fishermen relax on the beach trying to hold two children, one struggling, while they have their photo taken; the photographer has obviously told them to remain still for the exposure. They are sitting on a typical cove boat used for crabbing on the Lizard: she is wooden, carvel-built, a two master with lug sails being about 19 feet long. This is a nice early image of life in Cadgwith captured during the late 1870s.

Opposite below: This image is taken from a Victorian glass magic lantern slide. According to the contemporary title on the slide, it shows the injured being beached at Cadgwith from the wreck of the SS *Escurial*; sadly, eleven of her crew lost their lives in the wreck off Portreath, on the opposite coast of Land's End from Cadgwith. On the right-hand side of the image, there are two barrels and what appears to be a mattress, presumably salvage from the SS *Escurial*, which was wrecked on 25 January 1895. The Hayle lifeboat went to the rescue of the stricken ship; to do so; she was pulled 11 miles overland and launched at Portreath. It is curious that the conditions of the water in the image are flat calm; the SS *Escurial* was wrecked in a severe storm, and the fact Cadgwith is a long way from the wreck naturally brings doubt to all who have seen this photograph, so make up your own mind.

These two late Victorian photographs are of the *Victoria* being built and launched at Walter Cox's yard under Pendennis Castle on the River Fal. In 1899, William John Thomas in partnership with Arthur William Chard ordered the steamer, which was delivered in 1900. She was a twin-screw 82-feet long vessel, weighing in at 67.7 tons. Here above, we see her on the stocks on completion of building; the bottom photo shows her being launched with the Roseland Peninsula in the background. She was a ferry steamer and worked between Falmouth Truro and St Mawes.

A very early CdV of Pendennis Castle, which was taken by Falmouth professional photographer Frederick James Trull. This photo shows the Elizabethan fortress in 1863. The single-storied building with a porch and window was probably the guard room; this part has since been demolished.[53]

Above: This later image of Falmouth was captured on a magic lantern slide *c.* 1900; it shows a ketch purposefully grounded on Grove Place Beach. Astern of it are smaller boats running moorings attached to the quay wall. The row of terraced houses behind the ketch were built as private residences in the 1840s on Killigrew Estate land. The warehouse building to the far right is the present-day Trago Mills emporium. The beach has now been filled in and a water sports centre built in its place along with a car park furnishing the Maritime Museum and local shops.

Below: Falmouth Docks in the 1890s; in the larger No. 2 Dock sits the SS *Saint Enoch*. She was built in 1890 and she was launched in 1891 by Palmers Shipbuilding and Iron Co. Ltd at Tyneside for the British and Foreign Steam Ship Company. Her dimensions were a length of 375 feet, beam of 46.5 feet, and draft of 28 feet. She was broken up 1936. The docks were built in 1860, allowing ships from around the globe to take advantage of Falmouth's natural deep-water harbour.

Above: A very sharp CdV taken by Frederick James Trull of Falmouth, it shows the Falmouth Hotel very shortly after it was first built; the gardens have just been laid out and planted. The foundation stone was laid on 6 August 1863 by Robert Tweedy; it was opened on 9 May 1865 to accommodate the tourists that were arriving to the newly opened railway station. Apparently, the hotel cost a total of £9,000 to build.

Below: A view taken from a Victorian glass magic slide showing the Market Strand leading onto Market Street, Falmouth. In the background on the right, with meat hanging in the window, can be seen James Frederick Truscott's pork butchers and Ursula Millett's boot makers, which was in No. 3 Market Strand; her son William was also a boot and shoe dealer. Next to Millett's shop is Thomas Gooch tobacconists in No. 2 Market Strand; the neighbouring shop (No. 4) was Henry Liddicoat grocer and licensed victualler. This is a very vibrant scene, the street is bustling, and people standing looking at the camera, others are gossiping, and some are just out shopping. The photo was taken before 1891 when Thomas Gooch's entry in *Kelly's Directory* was omitted.

Above: A late nineteenth-century full-plate albumen print of the Moor, Falmouth; we are looking down Killigrew Street with the Methodist church on the right. On the left is the library, which was built in 1894 and is known as the Passmore Edwards Building. The memorial was erected by public subscription in memory of the gallant officers and men of HM Post Office Packet Service, sailing from Falmouth between 1688 and 1852.

Below: Falmouth County High School for Girls was built in 1887, Queen Victoria's Silver Jubilee year. The school was situated on the northern side of Western Terrace. The spotless, whitewashed walls and cleanliness of the building suggests this photograph was taken shortly after the completion of the building. It is interesting to see the weary donkey pulling the cart full of covered baskets down the hill.

Above: A late Victorian CdV of Flushing, which lies to the east across the Fal from Falmouth and was originally named Nankersey when the village was founded in 1661; the village's name was changed to Flushing by Dutch engineers who came from Flushing in the Netherlands and built the three main quays. This image is a general view of the quays and village from the river.

Below: A crystal-sharp full-plate albumen of a small cove on the River Fal; in the foreground is a thatched boathouse accompanied by an open timber boat shelter in the background; this image was taken by Falmouth photographer William Harrison in *c*. 1880.

This fantastic mounted and fully titled full-plate albumen of the building of the Cornwall Railways broad gauge Carnon Viaduct was taken by James Frederick Trull, who worked out of Falmouth. This amazing image must have been taken in 1862, a year before the Carnon viaduct was opened in 1863. This is a small cropped section of a much larger photo, but this shows the crane on rails that were used to manhandle the timbers fanning up off of the brick piers. The piers caused real problems as they had to be built through 20 feet of soft alluvium deposits from the local mines that formed soft mud flats on the Carnon riverbed. The viaduct was designed by I. K. Brunel and carried the Cornwall Railway line from Falmouth to Truro. The viaduct was a Class A viaduct: 96 feet high and 756 feet long. You can see the workmen standing precariously on the timber structure.

Above: A lovely full-plate albumen photo by Harrison of Falmouth taken in the late 1870s or early 1880s, this busy scene is looking south down Market Street, Penryn. The Methodist Chapel, which was built in 1881 and now dominates the lower part of the terrace, is notably absent in this photo. Penryn's distinctive clocktower dominates the centre of the scene and is part of the Town Hall, now the site of the town's excellent museum. The opposite side was then known as Fore Street but is now known as Market Street.

Below: A very interesting and unusual view is captured on this full-plate albumen of Broad Street, Penryn. This area was also known as 'Fish Cross' due to its proximity to the Fish Market. The Fish Market was in the open area on the right-hand side of the photo and was demolished during 1894 and 1895 with the old Fish Market cross that was situated there being moved next to the town hall in 1895. This photo was probably taken soon after the cross was removed; the fire station was built later during 1899. On the right-hand side of the photo can be seen a dray wagon delivering to the Kings Arms, which at this time was owned by George Chapman. To the left of the Kings Arms can be seen the Mechanics Institute. Across the street below the site of the old Fish Market can be seen a barber shop complete with pole; next door to this shop was a house occupied by the local general practitioner, Thomas E. Fisher, and in the large adjacent property lived Dr Blamey, a surgeon. The road was a hotchpotch of upper- and lower-class buildings and professions.

Above: Little is known about this albumen photo from the 1880s apart from the fact that it is annotated on the reverse: 'the Mayor of Penryn'. He is not wearing his official chain or robes, so he is presumably not on official business, making this a nice piece of Victorian social history.

Below: Built by the Cornwall Railway and designed by Isambard Kingdom Brunel, the Collegewood Viaduct is 0.25 miles south of Penryn. It is a Class A viaduct 100 feet high and 954 feet long. It was supported by fourteen brick piers supporting the wood, which fanned out above to carry the track; in 1934, this was the last timber viaduct to be replaced in Cornwall. This albumen print with Penryn in the background was taken around 1890.

A pair of very early stereoscopic slides sold by Spreat of Exeter, they would be sold under licence probably to Beringer of Helston. These are part of a series; a third one is shown on p. 31 of *Views and Likenesses* by the late Professor Charles Thomas. The cards are titled 'Freemans Granite Quarry, Carnsew near Penryn' and will date from the early 1860s. They show the granite being worked from the quarry walls. The wooden timber frames were called moulds and were used to give an approximate size of the block required. The cranes were then used to move the blocks onto carts, which would then be drawn down to Freemans Granite Quarry situated by the river at Penryn.

Above: This image, scanned from the original quarter-plate glass negative, shows the Penryn granite works on the banks of the Fal. Between 1840 and 1905 was the heyday for the John Freeman and Sons Granite Works of Penryn. By the 1880s, they employed 800 men. Cornish granite was used for lighthouses and bridges spanning the Thames. A team of horses can be seen bringing a block of granite to the works while in the centre of the workshops, huge blocks of granite are waiting to be worked on. There are men under the ramshackle corrugated iron canopy. Sadly, the firm petered out, partly due to the First World War; the buildings are now gone.

Below: An idyllic late Victorian view of Cowling's Creek, Kea near Truro on the Fal; apparently, the area is famed for being very rich in damson plums.

The *King Harry Ferry*, which plies between Feock and Philleigh on the River Fal; named after a King Henry, there is argument as to whether it is Henry VI or VIII. In 1888, a floating bridge was introduced; being steam-driven, it ran along a submerged chain, as does the present-day ferry, which can carry up to thirty-four cars. This photo was taken on the Feock side of the river before the chain ferry came into operation in 1888. The ferry carried vehicles with their accompanying horses; the ferry would have been rowed across the river to Philliegh, where the passenger and vehicle would disembark.[54] The cumbersome ferry in the photo was a horse ferry, which had hinged sections in the gunwales to help with boarding of the wagons and iron rings to tether the horses and secure the wagons; a smaller ferry would have been available for passengers on foot.

Truro during the mid-1880s. This photo was taken before the river was filled in and the various bridges built. One building everyone can identify is the old City Hall, which is now known as 'The Hall for Cornwall'. The rear of City Hall is the dark building to the right of Lemon Bridge; it was built as a concert hall with market and the council offices above. Towards Lemon Bridge and next to City Hall is the Market Inn. In 1900, the building to the right of the hall was demolished and replaced by N. Gill and Son's warehouse, which was designed by the prolific Cornish architect Silvanus Trevail. The pre Trevail building is the white stone one to the right of the ketch, which was moored alongside Back Quay. Back Quay stretched from Lemon Bridge to the end of the Bowling Green. The length of Back Quay from the white stone warehouse up to Lemon Bridge is also known as Market Strand. The white building facing the old bowling green was the Customs House; this was situated in Green Street, which derived its name from the bowling green. The large building to the right of the green was the Public Rooms, which were built in 1867. The construction of the new cathedral is evident with the scaffolding and cranes around it; it was consecrated for use in 1887. On the opposite bank of the river is Lemon Quay; the River Kenwyn comes down under the arched Lemon Bridge and joins the River Allen, which enters bottom right of the photo; from then on, they become the Truro river. The river frontage is very industrial at this time with baulks of timber, warehouses, long sheds, and a timber yard. Behind the very long low shed in the foreground with the chimney are what were the Trethellan Smelting Works; behind the smelting works are seen the gas works and gas holder (the round metal structure). This late Victorian scene is so very different from the Truro of today.

Lemon Street, Truro, named after the Lemon family who owned the land it was built on. This photo was taken from Lemon Bridge around 1870 or 1880. Lemon Street is a very wide and impressive steeply sloping street, which is lined with large houses built for the wealthy merchants during the early nineteenth century. The houses were of varying size, ranging from two and three-storey town houses mainly built of the local Newham stone. At the top of the hill can be seen the tall column—the Lander memorial—that was designed by architect Philip Sambell. Closest to the camera is Julian's Insurance Brokers first mentioned in *Kelly's Directory* of 1873. In the 1883 edition, it is shown as 'John Julians', so this full-plate albumen print was taken between those dates. Next to it is the home and business premises of the architect Silvanus Trevail.

These two photos are of Boscawen Street, named after the Boscawen family of Tregothnan. The street is so wide because there was another row of properties running down the centre of the road called Middle Row; these were demolished in the 1790s, this opened up a large space in the centre of the then town. As with several streets in Truro, Boscawen Street has charming granite setts and slab footways that were laid in the nineteenth century. The top photo is a cabinet card and the earlier of the two, taken before James Hicks and Silvanus Trevail completely remodelled the street; the lower photo is a CdV taken in the 1890s after some of the buildings had been changed. It is obvious that the wide street made ideal parking for the coaches and wagons with Boscawen Street being a five-minute stroll to all the commercial areas of Truro.[55]

The symmetrical seventeenth-century St Mary the Virgin's church; this CdV was taken in the 1860s by Frederick Argall from the east. The elaborately carved south aisle was incorporated into the present-day cathedral. The granite tower and spire were completed in 1796, measuring 125 feet; the clock was presented by Miss Carlyon. Most of the church and neighbouring properties were demolished when the present-day cathedral was built.

Above: Truro Cathedral probably taken in 1887 shortly after it was consecrated on 3 November for use as a cathedral but prior to the building of the spires. Construction continued from 1880 right through to 1910. It was designed by John Loughborough Pearson and built on the site of the sixteenth-century parish church of St Mary the Virgin. When St Mary's was demolished in 1880, the south aisle was retained to serve as a parish church during the building works; this was superseded by a temporary wooden building that could hold 400 people. The cathedral's 250-foot central tower and spire were completed in 1905 and the two 200-foot-tall Western towers were finished in 1910, completing the building works that took thirty years to complete.

Below: This albumen print shows the old Carvedras wooden trestle viaduct, one of the forty-two of the Cornwall railway viaducts made of yellow pine; the Cornwall Railway linked Plymouth to Falmouth and the Truro section was opened on 4 May 1859. This viaduct used to cross the fields that were later to be made into Waterfall Gardens in 1894, it was a Class A viaduct 86 feet high, 969 feet long, consisting of fifteen piers. In 1902, it was replaced by a stone viaduct, which is there to this day.

Above left: This albumen print taken only about twenty years after Union Place was built illustrates the genteel terraced streets being built in the Truro suburbs, near the River Allen and behind Philip Sambell's St Mary's Chapel; the side of the chapel can be seen far left of this photo. These terraced houses matched the quality of the best suburban developments. Union Place was typical of the better class residential buildings in Truro of the mid-nineteenth century with their rounded door arches and classical proportions.[55] Regrettably, this albumen print was badly pasted onto an album page and I was unable to illuminate the ripple effect.

Above right: An early CdV of a Truro senior fireman, indicated by his two stripes; he is wearing his leather helmet and carrying his axe. The photo was taken by Plymouth photographer John Palmer, who was working in Truro from 1857 to 1866.[56] There is not a lot more to be said about this image but the reader might be interested in this slightly later newspaper account of 1874 from the *West Briton and Cornwall Advertiser*:

> Capt. T. Olver, of Falmouth, at the Launceston Fire Brigade meeting, on Thursday, said that no doubt the Truro Fire Brigade was 'the best in the county'. He also stated that this was brought about mainly by the way in which the various authorities of that town, municipal and otherwise, acted together, and recognises further that the Launceston brigade had a 'very firm foundation', in the fact that they were cordially and warmly supported by the Mayor and Corporation.

Above: This is a late Victorian albumen print of Tregothnan taken about 1880; the house is 3 miles south-east of Truro and the ancestral home of the Boscawen family. The house is on the site of a medieval manor house that was decimated during the civil war; it was replaced with the present house in the mid-seventeenth century.

Below: This is probably the latest photograph in this book—the date stone at the top of the Probus Wesleyan School says 1901, the date the school was opened; however, when this photo was taken by Greet, the scene he captured shows a pile of stone by the gate, presumably to be used to finish the wall, also there are workmen in the schoolyard that had yet to be levelled, putting the date probably in 1901: shortly before the school was completed and opened.

Above: A very early CdV of the Henrician St Mawes Castle, this was probably photographed in the early 1860s, the sister fort to Pendennis Castle which was built on the opposite bank of the River Fal. This fort was built in the early seventeenth century, unlike Pendennis, which was little used and remodelled into barracks. Substantial gun batteries were built beneath it in the 1850s.

Below: An albumen print of St Mawes by Valentine, this image taken in the 1880s was prior to the building of the Star and Castle Hotel in 1900, changing the appearance of the frontage of the quay forever. In this photo, many of the ancient cottages are still thatched and other small whitewashed cottages line the streets. St Mawes Castle can be seen above the town and in the distance on the opposite bank of the River Fal is Pendennis Castle.

Above: Gerran's church, named after the eighth century Cornish King or Chieftain Geraint, who was converted to Christianity. The current church stands on the site of an earlier Celtic church; it was dedicated by Bishop Branscombe in 1261. It is built in the cruciform shape with a chancel, nave, and two transepts, with the tower at the western end. In the early fifteenth century, the steeple was added to form a landmark for the local fishermen and the building was enlarged. In the 1840s, the church caught fire and most of the roof was destroyed, forcing a renovation; six of the seventeenth-century carved bench ends were saved and thankfully, the parish registers dating from 1538 were rescued. There are several other interesting and original features that have been retained. This photo of the church was taken by H. T. Ashby in 1886.

Below: Another of H. T. Ashby's full-plate photos extracted from his photo album of 1886, this one shows Rosteague House, a medieval manor house with an Elizabethan façade. This house lies 1 mile from Gerrans village and looks out to sea; it is now privately owned and used for events.

Above: This is a beautiful photograph from H. T. Ashby's album of 1886 of a wagon and buggy outside the quaint thatched Trewithen Inn, which used to be at Trewithen near Portscatho; this charming building has long since gone.

Below: The heavily ivy-clad Tregassa Farmhouse in Porthscatho, its occupants are standing outside posing for the photo. The house has sixteen-pane sash windows with the lower floor windows taller than the upper floor ones. This photo was taken by H. T. Ashby in 1886.

These two photographs taken by H. T. Ashby are of Portscatho's seafront looking towards the harbour in 1886 prior to the breakwater being built; images of this village of this date are quite scarce so whoever H. T. Ashby was, I am grateful that he recorded the area in his precious album.

Above: A photograph of Portscatho before the breakwater, again taken by H. T. Ashby; in this image taken in 1886 we are looking back at the village. He must have been standing on the rocks by the sea; it is clear to see the way that the newly built houses are terraced down the slope and stretching out from the village so that all the mid-Victorian houses have a view of the sea, while the cottages in the old part of the village are huddled together, sheltered from the elements with no thought of the view.

Below: A late Victorian CdV of Portscatho harbour looking out to sea. A couple of old fishermen are working on their boats while up to the right can be seen some of the houses of the old village, one of which had a thatched roof. In the background can be seen the first breakwater. The breakwater was built in two stages; the initial building was by Mr Enys, the Lord of the Manor, after some of the protective rocks had to be cut away when the *Carl Hiracber* grounded there in the blizzard of 1891. A petition by the locals asked Mr Enys to extend the pier so steamers could moor alongside to facilitate the tourist trade. In 1912, an enquiry was put in place to try and extend the new pier by 200 feet and rake it inwards for the protection of the vessels in the harbour.

Above left: One of Portscatho's local characters captured sculling his 15-foot traditional clinker-built punt. He is called Jemmy and was photographed in 1886 by H. T. Ashby. Pictured wearing his knit frock with a local pattern on; apparently, it is said that from the pattern on the knit frock you could tell which village someone came from—this would have proved a great help with identification when a body was found.

Above right: H. T. Ashby photographed the local coastguard on patrol complete with telescope under his arm when posted as a lookout on the cliffs near Veryan. It is interesting to see his uniform: when this was taken in 1886, it is that of a naval seaman, yet the tally on the cap says coast guard.

Below: Two of Veryan's five roundhouses. There are two at each end of the village and one in the centre. They were built in the early nineteenth century by the Reverend Jeremiah Trist; all the Veryan round houses have thatched roofs with crosses on the top. H. T. Ashby obviously found them picturesque when he photographed them in 1886.

Above: A cob and thatch roofed cottage in a meadow right in the heart of Veryan village; I had great fun finding this cottage, which H. T. Ashby photographed in 1886. It is now called Fern Cottage and is located in the square opposite the New Inn. No longer does it have its thatched roof, and it has been extended, but if studied carefully, it can be seen that it is definitely the cottage in the photograph despite now having near neighbours.

Below: Taken by H. T. Ashby in 1886, this photograph is of Treworlas farmhouse. Treworlas is a hamlet between Ruan High Lanes and Pendower. The house is at the junction to Treworthal; opposite the house are two cottages, Dingles and Quince Cottages, which were originally called No. 1 and No. 2 Treworlas Cottages. Apparently at one time, part of the property was a public house; I have been told that when they slated the roof, they did so straight over the thatch.

Above: A cropped section of a CdV, it was taken by Redruth photographer James Moody in the 1860s of Caerhays Castle. The house is a walled manor house rather than a castle; the manor house had its origins back in the early thirteenth century. The estate is famous for its gardens and even at this early date, they look meticulously kept. Originally, the estate was owned by the Arundell family but after a few transfers of ownership, in 1854, the castle came into the hands of the present custodians: the Williams family.

Below: A mounted albumen photograph by Mitchell of St Austell, this foggy image was taken at Portmellon in 1886 and shows Mevagissey's ten-oared lifeboat. Her twelve-man crew are at their posts with oars at the ready, she is sitting on her carriage with no team of horses; members of the committee are standing by with their top hats on, everyone obviously posing for the photograph.

Sailing vessels are crammed into the dock at Charlestown. They are kept afloat by water being retained by the dock gates being closed and the ullage maintained by water brought from Luxulyan Valley through a leat. The vessel alongside the dock wall, centre of picture, is the *Vera*; these vessels at this time in during 1890s would have been exporting locally mined China clay.

Above: Charlestown Dock looking back towards the village. The dock gates can clearly be seen. Charlestown was built by Charles Rashleigh on the site of the small fishing hamlet of West Polmear. Work started in 1791 on a design by Smeaton of a dock and town to transport the copper ore from the local mines. After the 1850s, the copper trade slowed, and china clay became the main local cargo to be exported. On the right, shoots that were used to load the cargo can be seen; the hutches used to store the waiting copper ore can be seen in both photos. The left-hand side of the dock was used for the importation of coal and timber; the ships would be scrubbed spotless before being hauled across and filled with china clay. Charlestown is little changed to this day.

Below: This interesting industrial image was taken right on the cusp of the Victorian and Edwardian periods and shows what used to be Carclaze sawmills above St Austell, looking across at what is now Boscoppa towards Par. This area has now all been cleared and built on.

This is a CdV of the macabre practice of pig killing by St Blazey photographer T. Luke; when this photo was taken in the 1860s or '70s, pig killing was a necessity as most families had a pig that would be slaughtered to provide sustenance to the whole family, with cured meats such as bacon and ham, which would keep for months. Every part of the pig would be used and it was common custom in Cornish villages to pass meat around family and friends who lived in the locality; this would be a reciprocal arrangement. The pig was so important that many villages in the county had a pig club, which was like an insurance against the pig becoming ill, which would be disastrous for the welfare of the family.

Above: A mounted late Victorian albumen photo of an old cottage in Harmony Road, Roche. This quaint cottage was demolished in the 1960s.

Below: A full-plate albumen photo of Polkerris. Polkerris is a small fishing village on St Austell Bay, which lies 2 miles to the east of Fowey. The half-moon-shaped harbour wall was built in 1775 by the Rashleigh family to protect the seine boats, the villages main income was from the seine fishery for pilchards from the sixteenth century right up to the late nineteenth century.

Above: A late Victorian full-plate albumen print of St Catherine's Fort; the Henrician D-shaped building in the foreground was built in the 1530s by Thomas Treffrey with the River Fowey to defend against the threat of French attack. On the other side of the river is one of a pair of fourteenth-century blockhouses, one on each bank. These were part of the defences, having a chain running between them along the riverbed that could be raised to prevent ships from entering the river, protecting the port of Fowey; the vessels could then be attacked by the forts that were higher up the cliff face. Beyond the blockhouse is Polruan. Many sailing vessels are moored in the lee of the land, sheltered from the prevailing wind in Polruan Pool.

Below: Readymoney Cove on the River Fowey photographed in the later years of the 1890s. The cove's original name was Porth Mundy, which means 'mineral cove'; it lies just to the north of St Catherine's Fort, which can be seen on St Catherine's Point above the cove. In the early nineteenth century, it was used as a small shipyard. In 1792, pilchard cellars were built on the site of a former gun emplacement. The cellars were 52 feet long by 24 feet wide with walls being 2 feet thick. Above the cove and to the south is Point Neptune House. The cove has a small sandy beach and looks right across the river towards Polruan.

Above: Neptune Point House was built on the site of a Napoleonic gun battery above Readymoney Cove. This photo was produced as a stereoview soon after the renovations of 1862 by William Rashleigh of Menabilly. It is a forty-room mansion with beautiful panoramic views across the River Fowey; it was built of slate with granite dressings and slate roofs in the Victorian Italianate style.

Below: A beautiful early full-plate albumen photo of Fowey's parish church. The church is set in the heart of the town. The present-day church is on the site of an earlier Norman church, which was dedicated to Saint Finbarr in 1336. After damage by the French in 1457, the church was repaired and enlarged; the tower is of sixteenth-century construction. The font is Norman and carved out of Catacluse stone, a bluish grey hard stone quarried at Catacluse Point near Padstow and widely used for fonts, windows and church ornamentation at this time. Also notable are the fifteenth-century wagon roof, the hexagonal pulpit built in 1601, and the monumental brasses of the Rashleigh family.

Two photos of Fowey from the river, the top being a late Victorian mounted full-plate albumen by St Austell photographer W. Mitchell. It shows Fowey as if approaching the harbour from the seaward side; the sprawl from the medieval town can be seen along the bank of the River Fowey, in the distance can be seen Place House and the fourteenth-century parish church. The lower photo is taken from the north looking back down river towards the ancient quays and houses in this foggy albumen print from the 1880s.

Left: Fore Street, Fowey—an ancient street dating back to medieval times. One of the remaining ancient buildings is captured in this beautiful full-plate albumen print taken in the early 1880s of the Old Lugger Inn.

Below: A late Victorian photo of the horseferry that ran between Fowey and Bodinnick. Here we see the ferrymen rowing the boat using a pair of sweeps, one on the bow and one on the stern. The vessel is double ended and has a ramp at each end connected to a winch which could be used to lower the ramp for access to passengers and vehicles then raised again for the passage back across the river.

Two beautiful late Victorian photographs of Pont Quay. The top photograph is a view overlooking the quay and along Pont Pill towards the River Fowey at high tide. On the left can be seen a very large lime kiln and a small bridge across to the other cottages and warehousing on the quay. This creek had deep enough water that at high tide, sailing vessels could work up to these quays with cargo of culm and limestone for use in the lime kiln as well as other goods; culm is a lime-rich fine-grained type of coal. In the lower photograph, the tide is out and the tidal pool beyond the bridge is dry; there appears to be timber left in this pool to season.

A nice early CdV of Polruan probably taken in the late 1860s showing the shipbuilding port of Polruan; the town still carries on this trade even to this day with C. Toms Yard being a busy shipbuilding and repair yard.

An early CdV, probably from the late 1860s looking down the Fowey River, it was taken by W. Mitchell of St Austell. Vessels lay happily in the tranquil sheltered waters of Polruan Pool with the village of the same name laying away to the east.

Above: The quaint little fishing village of Polperro is nestled away in the valley, its harbour protected by the ancient quays. Note the staggered offset breakwater photographed in 1893, the reason for being staggered explained below. It is unknown when the first quays were built, but the inner quay walls are definitely the oldest ones, probably built in the sixteenth century; the outer quay walls, which are of an east–west alignment, were first built before 1774. These quays were badly damaged in 1817 when there was a violent storm where thirty large boats, two seiners, and many smaller boats were destroyed. Several houses were swept away in the tempest of 19 and 20 January, though thankfully there were no fatalities. In 1824, another terrifically powerful storm caused further devastation to the village, with three houses, one of the piers, and half of the other being swept away together with fifty boats that were in the protection of the harbour; only six boats survived the tempest. After this maelstrom, today's outer piers were rebuilt in the current staggered form.

Below: Polperro, again taken in 1893. It is hard to imagine over fifty boats packed into this little harbour for shelter. The Polperro gaffers are moored near the entrance to the harbour. Just right of centre is the bridge under which the River Pol emerges into the harbour. The quaint old cottages surrounding the harbour are quintessentially Cornish.

Above: This is a beautiful full-plate albumen photograph of the harbour at Polperro, looking from the Inner Quay out towards the sea. This photo was taken from outside the Three Pilchards Inn during the 1880s. A girl with a hoop and stick is leaning against the old wooden balances on the quay; these were used to weigh the fish.

Below: The ancient Crumplehorn cottages, Langreek Road, Polperro, photographed in August 1895; the house on the left has since been demolished and the cottage at the bottom of the row far right was called Sunny Corner. Crumplehorn was originally a separate hamlet from Polperro.

Above: An albumen print showing the thirteenth-century Talland Barton, Talland Bay, this photograph was taken in August 1895; the farmers of Talland Barton at this time were Richard and Ann Stephen.

Below: Taken in August 1895, this photo is looking up the river from Hannafore Lane towards East Looe. The low building on the front was called the Albatross and was a pilchard-packing factory. The building has long since been demolished and the present-day lifeboat station was built on the site; the original lifeboat station was the white building to the right.

Above: This beautiful photo was taken in August 1895 and is looking up West Looe Hill from the bottom. The cobbles seen lining the street were reputedly brought in as ballast on sailing vessels. The arched building on the left was a public well.

Below: This pair to the previous photograph was taken by the same photographer on the same August day in 1895. Here we are looking from Church Street towards West Looe Hill with the river behind you. The two ladies on the top of the steps to the right are members of the photographer's party appearing in other photographs in the album.

Above: A wonderful photograph taken in the 1880s showing West Looe on the left and neighbouring East Looe on the right. This part of the harbour was not the fishing port that is farther down river; this was the industrial area where heavy goods were moved by train and ships. Freeman's granite loading crane can be seen on the quay; this was used for lifting slabs of granite that were brought down from the quarries near the Cheesewring on Bodmin Moor onto waiting vessels. On West Looe Quay can be seen St Nicholas's church; next to it is a house that was later demolished to allow the road through to Hannafore to be built; this road was opened in 1895. Piles of coal brought by sailing vessels from South Wales can be seen on the quay; this was destined mainly to fuel the mines in the Minions area.

Below: Low tide at East Looe in 1893. Looking down river behind the beached ketch can be seen Looe's Banjo and Little Piers.

Above: Upriver at low tide looking towards Looe Bridge with West Looe on the left, taken in the mid- to late 1890s; this photo shows the granite crane at Freeman's Yard on the far right of the photo on Bullers Quay, East Looe. This quay was also known as Copper Ore Quay because when the mines at Minions were in production, the copper ore was transported from here to South Wales for smelting.

Below: Low water at Looe taken in 1893, looking across East Looe from Pennylands. On East Looe Quay can be seen the railway coal wagons; the coal was brought from South Wales by sailing vessel and then taken away by train to the local mines at Caradon or Minions.

Above: This photo of Bullers Quay was taken in the very last years of the nineteenth century. The road to Hannaford, which was opened in 1895, can be seen in the background; the Looe Hotel, which was built late in the century, stands proud opposite the Guildhall, which was built in the late 1870s, is obvious by its distinctive clock tower.

Below: A beautiful ships portrait of the sprit-rigged pleasure boat *The Pearl*. The sprit is the pole that held up the sail; in this photo, the sprit is on the far side of the sail. The man in the blazer was a tourist and part of the photographer's party who took this photo at Little Pier Looe in August 1895. These little sprit-rigged boats were traditionally used in the Looe and Gorran Haven areas for crabbing.

Above and below: A nice early pair of photos, probably from the 1870s, the top one showing the East Cornwall Hunt which is assembled a mile or so up river from Looe at Terras Bridge, the photo is probably taken from the railway line by the level crossing. The bridge was built in the mid-1800s to allow access to the Trenant Estate. In the bottom photo, between the boarding school and the bridge can be seen the old lime kiln; no trace of this lime kiln exists. The limestone was apparently brought down from Plymouth to be baked; the lime was used in various ways: for mortar, lime wash and also to be spread on the fields.

Above and below: In this albumen print dating from August 1895, we are looking west towards the Carlyon Arms; in the centre of this building is the present-day Carlyon House, which was built in the 1840s. The photo is looking along Loveny Road towards Loveny Bridge. The bridge crosses over the Loveny River, which meanders through St Neot. The river then goes on to feed the double overshot water wheels of St Neot Mill, which is situated just past the bridge on the left-hand side. Below is a close up of the north wall of the mill showing the then working water wheels.

Opposite below: Sandplace, located 2 miles from Looe up the East Looe River. The water that runs through the centre of the photo is the Moorswater to Looe Canal, which by this time was barely used being superseded by the railway; the tracks of which can be seen in the far left of photo. The house in the middle distance is called Polraen and was built of granite *c.* 1740; being on the main road between Liskeard and Looe, it is quite probable that this was originally a coaching inn; the building is now run as a small hotel.

Two late Victorian photographs of Lampen Farm situated in the Parish of St Neot. The photos have been included as they show a typical Cornish farmhouse and moway. The farm gets its name from the local family of Lampen: in 1610, there were only twelve men in the parish, one being William Lampen; in 1683, John Lampen transferred the family estate in fee simple to Lyne of St Cleer, moving to the Plymouth area but obviously the farm retained the name.

Two very early stereoviews distributed by Spreat of Exeter, they are both Cornwall Railway viaducts: the top one is Moorswater, taken in 1863, and the bottom one is Menheniot Viaduct, taken in the early 1860s. You will see the different construction used in each viaduct. Moorswater, the most spectacular of Cornish viaducts, was a Class B viaduct; it had a double fan on each pier and the timber laminated together between each fan to form a continuous beam. Menheniot, a Class A viaduct, had a fan shape on each pier but above it was a timber structure on which the track was mounted.

Camborne photographer William Sandry made the long journey up to Liskeard to take this cabinet card of Carwinion Terrace in the 1870s. Carwinion Terrace is next to Barnfield Terrace on Station Road, as is Manley Terrace pictured below, and captured on a full plate albumen print taken in the 1870s.

Two large photos taken by J. H. Coath of Lower Lux Street, Liskeard; both were taken in Castle Park, Liskeard recording the celebrations for the relief of Mafeking in May 1900. The man crouching down is Edward Borlase Wyndam Childs, the son of a Liskeard solicitor, Edward made the cannon; the event was covered in the local newspaper and this is an extract from the report:

> Fireworks were sent up from Castle Park at 9 o'clock. A novel feature of the celebrations was the firing of cannon at the castle green. It had been successfully manufactured from an iron pipe by Lieut. Childs V.B., D.C.L.I. Wm. Bright, Old Road; Liskeard received a slight wound in his leg during the firing of the cannon. He was removed to the Liskeard Cottage Hospital, and will be detained for a few days.

A marvellous mounted full-plate albumen taken by Gimbley Brothers of Gunnislake. The photo shows a local bus pulled by a team of four horses; five finely dressed ladies pose in front of the vehicle before mounting. The mind boggles as to where they were going to sit as the bus looks full to bursting with luggage on the roof, the driver proudly pulling at his braces looks like he will have plenty of cosy company on the journey.

Opposite above: A wonderful previously unpublished photo of Treveddoe Mine, Warleggan, near Liskeard. It was taken in August 1895. In the back can be seen the 24-foot pitch backwater wheel driven by water straight off of Bodmin Moor; this wheel drove the sixteen-head stamp batteries and tables seen to the right of the wheel. The ore would then be washed to classifiers worked by the same wheel. In the foreground of the photo are the circular round buddles. The concentrates and middlings feed material is brought for settling along the wooden launders to the central stone; the right-hand buddle is nearly full and would soon be ready to be emptied.

Opposite below: A CdV of St Cleer's holy well photographed shortly after its Victorian restoration in 1864. This granite ancient monument dating from the fifteenth century stands over a natural spring only a few feet away from an ancient Latin cross situated in the village of St Cleer. The quaint little building only measures approximately 12 feet by 18 feet and has pinnacles on each corner and one on the top of the front gable.

The following are a series of panoramic photographs taken by the Liskeard photographer J. H. Coath who had a holiday home in Downderry. He captured a lot of village life; these images are interesting for their unusual format, taken around 1900 and scanned from the original negatives. This image shows Hessenford just up the valley from Downderry

Another view of Hessenford.

Tommy Knight, flint napper, mending the road to Seaton; Seaton Bridge and lime kiln are in the background.

The same road as above, but this time we are looking in the opposite direction; Tommy Knight is seen on the left.

Looking towards Seaton beach, the old farm house can be seen in the foreground.

The main street in Downderry.

Moving the herd at Downderry.

On the beach at Downderry.

Downderry.

In Victorian times, the council paid a local man to break stone into smaller pieces to mend the holes in the roads. Here we see the Seaton road repairer John Knight, who lived up the valley at Hessenford. In two of the Seaton panoramic views, he can be seen on the same pile of stones situated on the Seaton Road not far from Seaton Bridge. The photograph was taken by J. H. Coath of Lux Road, Liskeard; he was a very arty photographer, and in this instance, I think he was trying to capture a parody between either rich and poor or old and young.

The Victorians were very fond of military type groups to instil discipline; the Boys' Brigade are a good example of this. These two photos are from a series of five images that capture life in the camp at Downderry in 1898. The top photo shows the boys in their full uniforms posing behind the mess tent; the lower photo shows them on parade facing the canteen. Behind the boys in the background can be seen Downderry's St Nicholas's church.

Inside the mess tent, the top photo shows the boys having their meal; and below, the officers at their table appear to be eating very well; a turkey, flowers for decorations, and nuts compared to the boys' meagre looking portions.

Above: The canteen complete with water barrel a bank of stoves with pots on, and galvanised baths for washing the dishes—quite an organised operation. They seem a relaxed and cheery bunch of men. Note the bugler calling everyone to mess far right of picture. The Boys' Brigade was founded in 1883 being the first voluntary uniformed youth movement in the world. The brigade brought camping into the calendar in 1886, making these photos very early in Boys' Brigade history; the brigade is still active to this day.

Below left: Taken by J. H. Coath of Liskeard, this photo shows a Victorian itinerant traveller with a dancing bear. The bear was on a chain and controlled with a long whip—a sight of a bygone era that luckily, we do not see in this day and age in this country.

Below right: This glass magic lantern slide taken *c.* 1900 is of Crafthole village in Sheviock parish. The slide is interesting as it shows the old market cross in its original position before it was moved to its present position on top of the hill; fairs were once held on the original site of the cross.

Above: This beautiful photo of Port Elliot and St Germans' church was taken in the 1880s. The house of Port Eliot is famous for its Tudor gateway; the house is purported to have been continuously lived in for over 1,000 years and claims to be the oldest continually inhabited dwelling in the UK. The house was remodelled in the eighteenth century by Sir John Sloane and is a listed Grade I priory and house. Right next door to the mansion is the church of St Germans; this Norman building has a wonderful carved contemporary doorway. The church is flanked by two imposing towers with Norman foundations; the church was the original cathedral of Cornwall from AD 926 where King Athelstan made Conan the first Cornish bishop. It is a truly remarkable pair of buildings on the banks of the River Tiddy.

Below: A nice albumen print from the 1880s, it shows William Gilbert's PS *Eleanor* working on the River Tamar at Calstock. The hotel on the right, which is framed by the woods of the Cotehele Estate, was called the Ashburton Hotel after Lord Ashburton, he owned vast swathes of land in the area; later renamed Danescombe Valley Hotel after the valley that can be seen running away from it into the distance.

A nice pair of photos of Rame church dated 1878. Rame church is dedicated to St Germanus, who was apparently a fighting German Bishop who came to Britain in 400. The original church was built in 1259; some parts of the original church still exist, including the slender un-buttressed tower topped with a broached spire. The church has fifteenth- and sixteenth-century additions. This church like most Cornish churches did not escape the Victorian restorers.

A pair of albumen prints taken in the 1880s of Cotehele on the banks of the River Tamar; a medieval house with Tudor additions, it is an imposing, rambling, ancient house and seat of the Edgecumbe family. The property was transferred from the family to the National Trust in place of death duties.

Above: A full-plate albumen print taken in the 1870s of the original eighteenth-century thatched Lady Emma's Cottage, which was destroyed by fire in 1880. It was rebuilt in 1882 in the arts and crafts style and was destined to later become a tea rooms.

Below: A very early albumen photograph of the Folly, built in approximately 1741 from ruined stone from the remains of St George's and St Lawrence's churches, Stonehouse. It was built on the Mount Edgecumbe estate overlooking the river Tamar to resemble a ruined church. Centre of the photo and in the mid background can be seen the fortifications on Drakes Island, which appear to be at quite an early stage with the walls being remarkably clean suggesting a date of perhaps before 1859 when the new programme of defences was suggested by a Royal Commission.

Two early photos of Mount Edgecumbe, the top one is showing a gentleman sitting with the house behind him it probably dates from the early 1860s; note the ha-ha to stop the sheep encroaching too close to the house. The bottom photograph was taken in the 1880s. Mount Edgcumbe was built as the family seat of the Edgecumbe's between 1547 and 1553 and was sadly badly damaged by the German bombing raids during the Second World War. The estate was sold to Cornwall County Council and Plymouth City Council in 1971 and has been open to the public since 1988.

Above: A very early stereoview of Picklecombe Cottages on the Edgecumbe Estate, this image probably dates from the late 1850s or early 1860s: only thirty or forty years after the pair of cottages were built. The outline and windows of the house are the same as today, though the main visual changes are the shingles that now cover the house were added after this image was taken. The cottages were part of the Edgecumbe estate and were built solely as an ornamental feature on the drive around the grounds.

Below: This wonderful albumen print was taken in the 1880s and shows some of the boys on board the TS *Mount Edgecumbe*, which was moored on the River Tamar. The ship was for homeless and destitute boys and she was licensed to carry 250 boys who lived on board. They had lessons in seamanship and other useful trades, such as shoe-making, as seen in this photo. Life on the ship was run on strict naval discipline—a real lifestyle change for these young boys, many of whom had been convicted of crime or found wandering. Life was run on a mess system where groups of boys would be put in various messes and they would have to learn to work together. The ship was on the River Tamar in the Saltash area from 1877 to 1920.[57]

These next four photographs are by the prolific Scottish photographer George Washington Wilson; he was so prolific that there is doubt as to whether he took all the photographs himself but could have used local photographer's images under license in his series of commercial views. The following four fascinating images are all of naval vessels on the River Tamar and taken during the early 1860s being sold as stereoviews.[58] Above is the sixteen-gun first-rate ship of the line, HMS *Cambridge,* on gun practice on the Hamoaze.

Below: The 104-gun HMS *Impregnable* on the Hamoaze; she was the original training ship 1862 to 1888.

Above: The 104-gun training ship HMS *Royal Adelaide* behind one of *Rendel's Floating Bridges*, which was inaugurated in 1834. These were the early steam ferries built to carry passengers and carriages and were designed by James Meadows Rendel.[59]

Below: The 104-gun first-rate ship of the line HMS *Royal Adelaide* on the Hamoaze, she was built in 1828.

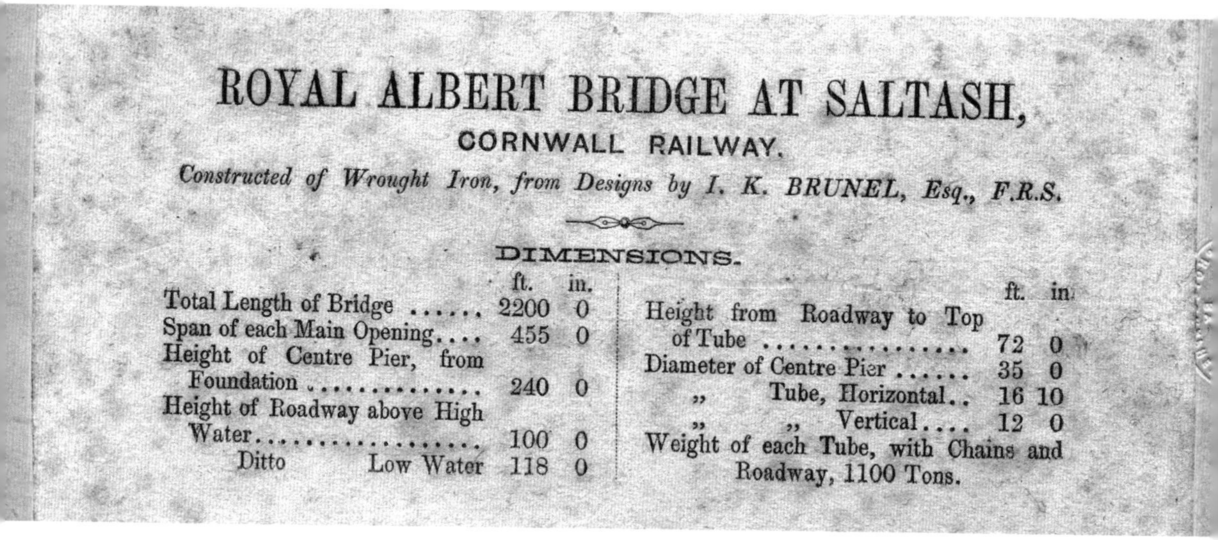

ROYAL ALBERT BRIDGE AT SALTASH,

CORNWALL RAILWAY.

Constructed of Wrought Iron, from Designs by I. K. BRUNEL, Esq., F.R.S.

DIMENSIONS.

	ft.	in.
Total Length of Bridge	2200	0
Span of each Main Opening....	455	0
Height of Centre Pier, from Foundation	240	0
Height of Roadway above High Water..................	100	0
Ditto Low Water	118	0
Height from Roadway to Top of Tube	72	0
Diameter of Centre Pier	35	0
,, Tube, Horizontal..	16	10
,, ,, Vertical....	12	0

Weight of each Tube, with Chains and Roadway, 1100 Tons.

Above: This is the back of a stereoview by William May of Devonport with details of the newly built Royal Albert Bridge. The front of the card has a very faded image of the bridge from Saltash Station taken very shortly after its opening on 2 May 1859.

Below: A stereoview of the Royal Albert Bridge, it was, taken in 1859 by Francis Luke. Who is the man standing proudly for the photograph wearing a stove pipe hat? At this time, Brunel was ill, so it is unlikely that it was him. In this view, we are looking across the Tamar towards Saltash.

Above: Another very similar stereoview to the previous image, both images were taken while the scaffolding was still in place in 1859. This view was sold by Spreat of Exeter.

Below: This third stereoview looking towards Saltash was probably taken by Luke on the same day as the previous image. The buildings in the foreground of all three images were sheds used in the construction of the bridge on the St Budeaux side of the river.

Above: One of a pair of full-plate albumen prints taken of the Royal Albert Bridge, this one is looking at it from the newly constructed Saltash railway station. The fences are clear of advertising signs and the old broad-gauge railway tracks are evident. On the pier below the bridge can be seen the 99-foot-long wooden paddle steamer *Fairy;* she was built in 1857 by a Stonehouse shipbuilder. After a long service, she was decommissioned and broken up in 1888.[60]

Below: The second of the pair full-plate albumen, this time looking back at Saltash from the Devon side of the bridge; both of these images were probably taken in the late 1860s. On the slipway at Saltash can be seen Saltash Floating Bridge No. 3 built during 1866 and 1867; its single funnel and central gangway can clearly be seen.[61] The earlier configuration of the vessel can be seen in the photo of *Rendel's Floating Bridge* on page 217; here the gangways were either side of a central steam engine, which pulled the ferry along a submerged chain.

By the time this CdV of Saltash station was taken, probably in the early 1870s, advertising had started to appear on the railings. The broad gauge is still being used, but the station is little changed from the earlier image showing the bridge behind it.

This very grainy CdV was taken by Groom of Plymouth and again shows a view of the Royal Albert Bridge. It was well photographed at this time, being an astonishing piece of engineering. We are looking from Station Road, Saltash, towards Devon. Studying the lady's costume, it must have been taken in the late 1850s or early 1860s, just after the completion of the bridge.

Endnotes

1. Thorn, *Thorns of Bude* (2016), p. 32.
2. *Ibid.*, p. 87.
3. *Ibid.*, p. 86.
4. McCarthy, *Cornwall from Magic Lantern Slides* (2016), p. 18.
5. Thorn, *Thorns of Bude* (2016), p. 37.
6. *Ibid.*, p. 86.
7. *Ibid.*, p. 19.
8. *Ibid.*, p. 30.
9. *Ibid.*, p. 30.
10. *Ibid.*, p. 36.
11. Venning & Wills, *Yesterday's Town Launceston* (1988), p. 15.
12. Thorn, *Thorns of Bude* (2016), p. 95.
13. Knight & Knight, *The Book of Boscastle,* (2004), p. 94.
14. Boquet, *Westcountry Sail* (1971), p. 41
15. Thomas, *Views and Likenesses* (1988), p. 96.
16. McCarthy, *Padstow* (1994), p. 34.
17. *Ibid.*, p. 35.
18. Raymont, *Padstow in the Mid-nineteenth Century* (1989), p. 118.
19. *Ibid.*, p. 6.
20. *Ibid.*, p. 68.
21. McCarthy, *Padstow* (1994), p. 56.
22. Raymont, *Padstow in the Mid-nineteenth Century* (1989), p. 67.
23. *Ibid.*, p. 68.
24. *Ibid.*, p. 10.
25. *Ibid.*, p. 104.
26. McCarthy, *Padstow* (1994), p. 62.
27. Raymont, *Padstow in the Mid-nineteenth Century* (1989), p. 127.
28. Thomas, *Views and Likenesses* (1988), p. 29.
29. *Ibid.*, p. 120.
30. *Ibid.*, p. 145.
31. *Ibid.*, p. 43.
32. *Ibid.*, p. 123.
33. Searle, *One & All* (2005), p. 101.
34. Thomas, *Views and Likenesses* (1988), p. 99.
35. *Ibid.*, p. 29
36. *Ibid.*, p. 44.
37. *Ibid.*, p. 113.
38. *Ibid.*, p. 116.
39. *Ibid.*, p. 32.
40. Watkins, *Early Photographs of the West Cornwall Peninsula* (1978 reprint), p. 108.

41. *Ibid.*, p. 91.
42. *Ibid.*, p. 2.
43. Thomas, *Views and Likenesses* (1988), p. 151.
44. *Ibid.*, p. 52.
45. *Ibid.*, p. 52.
46. *Ibid.*, p. 79.
47. Benny, *Cornish watermills* (1972), p. 51.
48. Orchard, *Penzance in Old Picture Postcards* (1982).
49. Thomas, *Views and Likenesses* (1988), p. 108.
50. *Kelly's Directory* (1856), p. 33.
51. Thomas, *Views and Likenesses* (1988), p. 74
52. *Ibid.*, p. 83.
53. *Ibid.*, p. 135.
54. McCarthy, *Cornwall from Magic Lantern Slides* (2016), p. 99.
55. Kirkham, *Cornwall and Scilly Urban Survey. Historic Characterisation for Regeneration. Truro,* (2003), numerous.
56. Thomas, *Views and Likenesses* (1988), p. 150.
57. Hunt, *TS Mount Edgecumbe,* general.
58. Thomas, *Views and Likenesses* (1988), p. 138.
59. Kitteridge, *Rendel's Floating Bridges* (2008) p. 48
60. Kitteridge, *Steamers and Ferries of the River Tamar* (2003) p. 33
61. Kitteridge, *Rendel's Floating Bridges* (2008) p. 90